The Inner Compass

The Inner Compass

Navigating life's journey with insight and direction

Dr. Shirish M. Narsapur

"कर्मण्येवाधिकारस्ते मा फलेषु कदाचन। मा कर्मफलहेतुर्भूर्मा ते सङ्गोऽस्त्वकर्मणि॥"

Bhagavad Gita: Chapter 2, Verse 47

"You have a right to perform your prescribed duties, but you are not entitled to the fruits of your actions. Never consider yourself to be the cause of the results of your activities, nor be attached to inaction."

Dedication

To my wife Sumathi, daughter Shastha, son Satvik, and my mother Malati.

In loving memory of my father, (late) Dr. Madhusudan S. Narsapur.

To my close family, Jayateerth and Kusuma Koty (Parent-in-laws), Puneet, Snehal, Venkatesh, Shalini, Ram, Aruna, Pranshu, Pratyay, Stavya, Ahana and relatives from the entire Narsapur, Karalgikar, Tenglikar and Koty families for their endless support and love.

To my teachers, Dr. Dinshaw Pardiwala for teaching me my passion and Dr. Ramnath Ghute, for making me able to follow my passion.

To my doctor friends, who have always been there for me: My closest friends—Dhaval, Pavan, Gautham, and Vijay

And all my dear friends—Sheetal, Sachin, Ranjith, Thej, Pinaki, Ashwini, Jyoti, Nimish, Ashish, Mandar, Chinmaya, Subbaiah, Narayan, Lingaraj, Ashraf, Niyaz, Wajid, Omkar, Bhim, Rashmi, Raghu, Makarand, Parag, Anuj, Seema, Kavita, Manisha, Prachi, Deepak, Gaurang, Vinod, Dhiraj, Darshan, Priya, Pankaj, Jignesh, Daksha, Virat, Satish, Sandeep, Aneeta, Mallesh, Yuvaraj, Neelesh, Shankar, Nachiket, Felice, Akshay, Amol, Rajiv, Ketki, Shweta, Sameer, Deepa, Raghav, Rajendra, Rajeev, Milan,

Eswaran, Rajaram, Deepthi, Joticaa, Rupali, Anil, Vishwanath, Subhash, Nitin, Bhavinkumar, Channa, Sujal, Ankit, Anand, Mamta, Raghuraj, Prajakta, Kedar, Bhavesh, Shantanu, Kumar, Santosh, Goviind, Janak, Yusuf, Ranjan, Zakir, Lokesha, Rajat, Pranav, Shamik, Shaukat, Rutul, Nikesh, Divyesh, Mahesh, Sushil, Pradip and all my friends from Med school & the "Katta" group on Wealthcon—for always providing positivity.

Special thanks to Dr. Munjal Pandya for inspiring me to publish my book and Dr. Ronak Patel for the beautifully designed cover page.

Preface

In a world that often moves too fast, where the noise of daily life can drown out our inner voice, I found solace in words. Words have the power to inspire, to lift us when we are down, and to provide clarity in moments of doubt. This book is a collection of such words—quotes that I have crafted over time, each born out of individual experiences, observations, and reflections on life, work, character, and the human spirit.

While this collection may be modest for now, each quote holds a deep significance. They represent moments of clarity, lessons learned, or simple truths that emerged from the complexities of life. My hope is that these quotes resonate with you, offering the same comfort and inspiration they provided me, and that they serve as gentle reminders of the strength and positivity that reside within each of us.

This book is more than just a compilation of thoughts; it is a conversation between you and me. A dialogue about the values that shape our lives, the character that defines us, and the work that fulfills us. As life continues to unfold, I hope to add more to this collection, expanding it with new insights and reflections. Future editions will hopefully bring even more quotes that reflect the evolving journey we all share.

Thank you for allowing my words to be a part of your journey. May this book inspire you to reflect, to grow, and to embrace the positivity that life has to offer.

Dr. Shirish M. Narsapur

Contents

Introduction

In the tapestry of human experience, words are the threads that weave our thoughts, emotions, and actions together. They carry the power to uplift, to console, to challenge, and to inspire. As I embarked on the journey of drafting this book, I was continually reminded of how profound an impact a single sentence can have on a person's life.

This book is a collection of quotes that I have crafted, inspired by the experiences that have shaped me, both personally and professionally. As a practicing orthopedic surgeon with a special focus on sports medicine and joint reconstructions, I have had the privilege of collaborating closely with individuals who have faced both physical and mental challenges. This unique perspective has deepened my understanding of resilience, perseverance, and the human spirit's capacity to overcome adversity. These experiences have informed many of the quotes in this book, reflecting the intersection of life's challenges and the strength needed to navigate them.

Why Quotes?

You might wonder, why a book of quotes? In an age of information overload, where we are constantly bombarded with words from all directions, why choose to focus on something so concise? The answer lies in the unique power of a well-crafted quote. Unlike lengthy discourses or elaborate essays, a quote cuts through the noise. It distills wisdom into its purest form, offering it in a way that is easy to grasp, yet profound in its implications. Quotes can linger in our minds, to echo in our thoughts long after we have encountered them. They can be revisited, contemplated, and applied to various aspects of our lives. In just a few words, they can encapsulate complex ideas, provoke deep introspection and motivate action.

This is why I have chosen to share my thoughts in this format—because I believe that a single line can sometimes say more than an entire chapter.

The Journey of Creation

Creating these quotes has been a deeply personal journey. Each one has its own story, its own origin. Some were born in moments of quiet reflection, others in the midst of life's storms. There were times when the words flowed effortlessly, as if they were already waiting to be discovered. At other times, they emerged slowly, painstakingly, as I grappled with the lessons that life was teaching me.

This collection is, therefore, not just a book of quotes; it is a record of my journey through life, both in and out of the operating room. It captures my thoughts on various subjects—life, work, character, and human experience. It is an ongoing project, one that will grow and evolve as I continue to navigate the complexities of existence. The quotes in this book represent my current understanding, but I look forward to adding more as I gain new insights and perspectives.

Themes and Reflections

The quotes in this book are grouped around several key themes—life, work, character, and more. Each theme represents a different facet of our existence, yet they are all interconnected. Life is the overarching canvas, work is one of the primary ways in which we express ourselves, and character is the foundation upon which everything else is built. Each quote has been expanded into a short chapter, one that not only explains the quote but also affirms its true essence and application in life. The application can be individually catered to as different professions require different arrangements.

Through these quotes, I hope to offer you not just inspiration, but also a framework for thinking about these important aspects of life. For instance, in the section on life, you will find quotes that explore the essence of living fully, embracing change, and finding meaning in everyday experiences.

The section on work delves into the importance of passion, perseverance, and purpose in what we do. And in the section on character, you will encounter reflections on integrity, resilience, and the moral compass that guides us. Words in the book thus have been repeated multiple times which may sometimes feel redundant, but I assure you, they are not. It is my belief that repetitive use of certain positive words will force the reader to feed in the positivity that I aim to create via this book.

Each quote is a seed, and it is up to you, the reader, to plant it in the soil of your own life. As you reflect on these quotes, I encourage you to think about how they apply to your own experiences, your own challenges, and your own journey.

A Living Collection

It is important to note that this book is not a finished product. It is a living collection, one that I hope to expand in future editions. As I continue to grow and learn, I will undoubtedly encounter new insights and uncover new truths that will find their way into these pages. My hope is that this book will grow alongside you, offering new perspectives and inspiration with each edition. Most importantly, these quotes were self-written although a few have been inspired though not exactly duplicated from other published stories. Each quote was searched for exactly as they were conceived to confirm that these are not plagiarized in any way.

In the end, this book is as much about you as it is about me. It is an invitation to embark on a journey of self-discovery, to find inspiration in the ordinary and extraordinary moments of life. I hope that these quotes will serve as companions on your journey, providing guidance, encouragement, and, most importantly, a reminder of the incredible strength and potential that lies within you. There is a separate section of notes at the end of this book to help you jot down points that can help you tune your inner compass. This has been done deliberately and not just to fulfil the page needs.

Thank you for joining me on this journey. I am honored to share these words with you, and I look forward to the many editions that will follow, each one a testament to the ongoing adventure of life.

Dr. Shirish M. Narsapur

Quote 1

"Be good. Not just as good as you can be, but as good as good can be."

Chapter 1

The Relativity and Quantification of Goodness

The good and the bad are relative terms but, at the same time, quantifiable. In the column of good comes better and best, while in the bad comes worse, to assess the quantification. What defines a good or bad is not always based on comparison but by its inherent nature. To utterly understand this concept, one must delve deeper into what it means to be "good" and why striving to be "as good as good can be" is more than a simple goal—it's a fundamental philosophy for life.

To be good is not merely to be adequate or to meet a minimal standard. It is not about being "good enough" by someone else's standards or even by our own limited understanding of goodness. Instead, it is about striving to embody goodness in its purest form, in all actions, thoughts, and intentions. This aspiration involves a relentless pursuit of virtue, not just achieving a level of goodness that is comfortable or convenient but pushing beyond one's limits to reflect the highest possible standard of what good can be.

Understanding Goodness Beyond Relativity

Goodness, in its truest form, is not simply a matter of being better than something bad. It is not a mere absence of malice or wrongdoing. It is an initiative-taking commitment to doing what is right, to embodying values that transcend self-interest, and to contributing positively to the world around us.

Goodness is characterized by qualities such as empathy, integrity, humility, compassion, honesty, and fairness. It is not about the superficial acts of kindness performed for recognition but the deep, often unnoticed acts of generosity, love, and selflessness that define a person's true character.

While societal norms and cultural contexts can shape our understanding of what is good or bad, there are universal principles of goodness that stand the test of time. These principles are based on the inherent nature of actions—whether they promote love, peace, justice, and respect for all beings, or whether they contribute to harm, division, and suffering.

Why Strive for Goodness and Not the "Best"?

It might seem that aiming for the "best" would be the ultimate goal, but focusing on being "good" holds a more profound significance. When we strive to be "as good as good can be," we leave room for continuous growth and improvement. Goodness has an inherent humility; it acknowledges that there is always room for betterment, for deeper understanding, and for more compassionate action.

On the other hand, when the mind starts believing it has achieved the "best," complacency often follows. The idea of being "best" suggests a finality—a peak beyond which no progress is necessary or even possible. This mindset can stifle growth, limit creativity, and breed arrogance. The sense of having reached the ultimate level may lead one to stop reflecting, learning, and striving to be better.

Goodness, however, is an open-ended pursuit. It does not set a limit on virtue or excellence. Instead, it continually challenges us to look within, to see how we can be more honest, kinder, more understanding, and more courageous. Goodness is dynamic and ever evolving, while "best" can become stagnant and self-satisfied.

Philosophical and Cultural Perspectives on Goodness

Throughout history, the idea of goodness has been explored by many thinkers, philosophers, and spiritual leaders. Aristotle, for instance, spoke of the concept of "eudaimonia," or human flourishing, which is achieved not by a single act but through a life lived in accordance with virtue. According to Aristotle, goodness is a continuous pursuit of moral excellence—a habit rather than an endpoint. This helps us align with the idea of striving to be "as good as good can be," where the focus is not on reaching a state of perfection but on consistently practicing virtues such as courage, temperance, and justice.

Similarly, in Eastern philosophy, Confucius emphasized the importance of "ren," often translated as benevolence or humaneness. Confucius taught that a genuinely good person acts out of compassion and empathy, always seeking to do what is right for others. This idea resonates with the concept of expanding one's understanding of goodness beyond personal achievements to encompass a broader responsibility to the community and humanity as a whole.

Modern Context and Relevance: Goodness in Today's World

In today's world, the pursuit of goodness can sometimes feel like swimming against the current. We live in a time where success is often measured by wealth, status, or social media followers—metrics that do not necessarily correlate with being good. Yet, the need for goodness has never been greater. In an era marked by social and political divisions, climate change, and widespread inequality, individual acts of goodness have the power to create meaningful change.

Goodness in a modern context means using our resources, voices, and actions to uplift others, promote justice, and contribute to a fairer, more compassionate world. It is about standing up against injustice, being a voice for the voiceless, and choosing integrity over convenience.

The Inspiring Example of Jadav Payeng: Striving for Goodness Beyond Recognition

Jadav Payeng, known as the "Forest Man of India," is a powerful example of someone who has embodied the principle of being "as good as good can be." Over the past four decades, Payeng has single-handedly transformed a barren sandbar in the Brahmaputra river into a lush, thriving forest that spans over 1300 acres.

His journey began in 1979, when he noticed the severe erosion and destruction of natural habitat on Majuli Island, one of the world's largest river islands. While many might have considered the task impossible or left it to governmental agencies, Payeng took it upon himself to plant trees—one at a time—nurturing them daily, often against great odds. His work has provided shelter for wildlife, improved the local ecosystem, and even helped combat climate change in the region.

Payeng's dedication did not stem from a desire for fame or recognition; he started his mission quietly, without expecting any reward or acknowledgment. His actions exemplify goodness in its purest form—performed not for accolades but for the inherent value of contributing positively to the world. His story teaches us that true goodness is defined not by the magnitude of the action but by the intention and commitment behind it.

Jadav Payeng did not strive to be "the best" environmentalist. Instead, he focused on being "good" by doing what he could, day after day, to restore life to a dying landscape. His work is a testament to the transformative power of continuous, humble effort—an example of being as good as good can be.

Practical Steps Toward Being "As Good as Good Can Be"

So, how do we strive for this ideal of goodness in our everyday lives? Here are a few practical steps:

1. Practice Empathy: Make an effort to understand and share the feelings of others. Empathy allows us to connect with people on a deeper level, fostering kindness and understanding.

2. Choose Integrity: Make decisions based on ethical principles, even when no one is watching. Integrity builds trust and respect and is a cornerstone of true goodness.

3. Proactive in kindness: Look for opportunities to help others.

Whether those helps are through small acts like offering a kind word or larger efforts like volunteering your time or resources is immaterial.

1. Reflect Regularly: Take time to reflect on your actions, motivations, and decisions. Ask yourself, "Am I striving to be as good as good can be, or am I settling for 'good enough'?"

2. Cultivate Gratitude: Appreciate the goodness in others and in yourself. Recognizing the good in life can inspire us to contribute more positively to the world around us.

Reflection Questions:

1. When was the last time you chose goodness over convenience? How did it impact you and those around you?

2. What are some areas in your life where you feel you could strive for greater goodness?

3. How do you oversee situations where goodness may seem impractical or difficult?

Conclusion: An Ongoing Journey

Goodness is not a final destination but an ongoing journey. It is a commitment to self-betterment, ethical living, and positive impact. It is about striving to be not just "as good as we can be" but "as good as good can be"—embracing the ever-present possibility of growth and the boundless potential for kindness and compassion.

By committing to this path, we not only enrich our own lives but also contribute to a world that is kinder, more just, and more connected. So, let us strive each day to be a little better, a little kinder, and a little more understanding. Let us choose to be as good as good can be so that our inner compass always points in the right direction.

Quote 2

"Humility is what defines the character."

Chapter 2

Understanding Humility: The Foundation of True Character

Humility is often misunderstood as a sign of weakness, passivity, or self-deprecation. Humility is one of the most profound strengths a person can possess—a quality that enables us to see ourselves and others with clarity, fairness, and grace. It is the ability to recognize our limitations, acknowledge our mistakes, and remain open to learning and growth. Humility is not about thinking less of us but about thinking of ourselves less. It involves a realistic assessment of our strengths and weaknesses, knowing that we are not infallible and that there is always room for improvement.

To be humble is to be free from arrogance, pride, and self-centeredness. It is to approach life with a mindset that values learning over knowing, service over status, and empathy over judgment. Humility is the cornerstone of true character because it enables us to act with empathy, integrity, and authenticity. It allows us to build meaningful relationships, lead with wisdom, and contribute positively to the world around us.

Why Humility Defines Character

1. Openness to Growth and Learning:

Humility allows us to remain open to current ideas, perspectives, and experiences. When we acknowledge that we do not know everything, we create space for continuous learning and growth. A humble person does not see criticism or failure as threats to their ego but as opportunities to gain experience and evolve.

People who practice humility are more likely to seek feedback, listen actively, and adapt their behaviors based on what they learn. This willingness to learn from others, admit mistakes & correct them is a hallmark of true character and maturity.

2. Building Trust and Respect:

Humility fosters trust and respect in all kinds of relationships. A humble person does not feel the need to dominate or belittle others; instead, they treat everyone with respect and kindness, regardless of status or power. This quality makes them more approachable and relatable, as they are genuinely interested in others' perspectives and value their input.

In leadership, humility is crucial. Humble leaders inspire confidence and loyalty because they lead by example, demonstrating that they are willing to learn and grow alongside their team. They do not seek personal glory but aim to uplift and empower others.

3. Promoting Empathy and Compassion:

Humility is deeply connected to empathy and compassion. When we are humble, we are more likely to recognize the struggles and strengths of others. We become less judgmental and more understanding, fostering a sense of connection and community.

A humble person understands that everyone has something to contribute and that their worth is not diminished by the successes or failures of others. This perspective fosters a sense of equality and mutual respect.

Misconceptions About Humility

Humility is often misconstrued as passivity or lack of self-confidence. Some believe that humble people allow themselves to be walked over or fail to assert their own needs and rights. However, true humility is not about diminishing oneself; it is about recognizing one's worth while simultaneously valuing the worth of others.

Its also essential to distinguish humility from humiliation. Both are two entirely different things, even though it's easy to confuse them. Humility is a voluntary act of recognizing our limitations, being open to learning, and respecting others. It is a choice that reflects strength, maturity, and self-awareness. Humiliation, on the other hand, is an involuntary experience of being demeaned or belittled by others. It is often imposed upon a person, causing pain, shame, and a sense of inferiority.

Humility empowers; humiliation disempowers. While humility fosters growth, learning, and self-respect, humiliation often results in feelings of resentment, defensiveness, and diminished self-worth. Therefore, embracing humility should not be seen as accepting humiliation. Humility is about choosing to be grounded and open-minded, whereas humiliation is an attack on one's dignity.

Nelson Mandela: A Paragon of Humility in Leadership

A shining example of humility in leadership is Nelson Mandela, who, despite enduring 27 years of imprisonment, emerged without bitterness or a desire for revenge. Instead, he chose a path of reconciliation, forgiveness, and humility, which defined his leadership style and his legacy.

When Mandela became the first Black president of South Africa in 1994, following the end of apartheid, he was thrust into a position of immense power. Given his history and the decades-long oppression suffered by the Black population, it would have been understandable if he had chosen to exact revenge or sought retribution against the apartheid regime and its supporters, especially the Afrikaners who had enforced the system of racial segregation and discrimination.

However, Mandela displayed remarkable humility. He understood that his personal power was not for wielding authority or seeking vengeance but for healing a divided nation. He knew that the end of apartheid was not the end of the struggle but a new beginning.

It was the start of a long journey towards unity and reconciliation.

Humility in Action: Mandela and the 1995 Rugby World Cup

One of the most profound examples of Mandela's humility was his approach to the 1995 Rugby World Cup, held in South Africa just a year after he became president. Rugby had been seen as a symbol of apartheid, primarily supported by the white Afrikaner community. The national team, the Springboks, was predominantly white and had long been regarded as a symbol of white supremacy.

Mandela saw the potential for rugby to become a unifying force for the nation. Despite the sport's association with apartheid, he chose to embrace it as a means of reconciliation. Instead of alienating the Afrikaners, he wore the green and gold jersey of the Springboks—an act of profound humility and empathy.

Mandela understood that to truly lead South Africa into a new era, he needed to win over not just the oppressed Black majority but also the former oppressors. By officially supporting the Springboks, he demonstrated his willingness to set aside past grievances and extend a hand of friendship to the Afrikaner community.

His actions sent a powerful message to all South Africans: that they were united in their diversity and that the future belonged to everyone, regardless of race or past divisions. This gesture of humility was not just symbolic; it had a profound impact. It inspired the Springboks to victory, defeating the formidable New Zealand All Blacks in the final, and it brought South Africans of all races together in a moment of shared pride and celebration.

The Transformative Power of Humility

Mandela's humility did not just change the course of a rugby game; it changed the course of a nation. By refusing to seek revenge or assert dominance, he laid the groundwork for peace, understanding, and mutual respect. He showed that the true leadership is not about asserting power or seeking glory but about serving others and promoting unity.

Mandela's decision to support the Springboks, despite their history, demonstrated his understanding that humility is not weakness; it is strength. It takes strength to forgive, to empathize, and to reach out to those who were once considered enemies. It takes courage to put aside personal grievances for the greater good. Through his actions, Mandela showed that humility is not just a personal virtue; it is a powerful tool for social change.

Applying Humility in Everyday Life

While not everyone may face the same monumental decisions as Mandela, the principle of humility applies in every aspect of our daily lives. Here are some practical ways to cultivate humility:

1. Listen More, Speak Less: Practice active listening in conversations. Show genuine interest in what others have to say and be willing to learn from their experiences.

2. Admit Mistakes: Be open about your mistakes and take responsibility for them. Instead of justifying or downplaying errors, acknowledge them honestly and seek ways to correct them.

3. Celebrate Others' Successes: Recognize and celebrate the achievements of others without feeling threatened or envious. Understand that their success does not diminish your worth.

4. Seek Feedback: Repeatedly ask for feedback from others and be open to constructive criticism. Use it as an opportunity for growth, rather than taking it as a personal attack.

5. Serve Others: Look for ways to serve others, whether through volunteer work, helping a friend in need, or simply offering kindness to a stranger. Service fosters empathy and reminds us that we are part of a larger community.

Reflection Questions:

1. When have you practiced humility in your life? What impact did it have on you and others?

2. Are there situations where you find it challenging to be humble? Why, and how can you approach these situations differently?

3. How can you use humility to build stronger, more authentic relationships with those around you?

Conclusion: Humility as a Defining Virtue

Humility is not about self-effacement or denying one's strengths; it is about acknowledging those strengths while remaining open to learning, growth, and the value of others. It is the key to true character because it fosters empathy, respect, and trust—qualities that are essential for meaningful relationships and effective leadership.

Nelson Mandela's example teaches us that humility has the power to transform not just individuals but entire communities and nations. His humility in leadership brought healing to a divided country and created a foundation for lasting peace. We may not all be called to lead nations, but we can all strive to lead our lives with humility.

By embracing humility, we not only define our character but also strengthen our inner compass to help contribute to a more compassionate, just, and united world.

Quote 3

"*Accepting criticism builds a stronger self then just accepting appreciation.*"

Chapter 3

Two Sides of the Same Coin: Criticism and Appreciation

There is a popular saying that "criticism and appreciation are two sides of the same coin." Both are integral to our personal and professional growth, yet they play distinct roles. Appreciation affirms what we have done right, providing encouragement, and boosting confidence. On the other hand, criticism, especially when constructive, highlights areas that require improvement, serving as a catalyst for growth and development. While appreciation is undoubtedly valuable, it is through criticism that we often find the greatest opportunities to evolve.

Converting Criticism into Future Appreciation

To truly grow and develop, one must learn to accept criticism and use it constructively. Criticism is like a mirror—it reflects not just our strengths but also our blind spots and weaknesses. When we take criticism positively, it can become a powerful tool to sharpen our skills, refine our character, and drive us toward excellence. By embracing criticism and acting upon it, we set ourselves on a path where today's criticism can be transformed into tomorrow's appreciation.

The Dangers of Only Accepting Appreciation

While appreciation can be motivating, it also has a potential downside. When we focus solely on appreciation and ignore criticism, we risk becoming complacent or even arrogant. The belief that we have "arrived" or that we are beyond reproach can lead to stagnation, a lack of growth, and even a decline in performance. Genuine strength comes not from basking in praise but from facing and overcoming the challenges and flaws that criticism reveals. This means any sort of criticism be it positive or negative.

The Role of Positive and Negative Criticism

Criticism comes in two forms: positive (constructive) and negative (destructive). Positive criticism aims to build up; it is delivered with empathy and a genuine desire to help someone improve. It offers specific feedback, identifies areas for growth, and suggests practical steps for improvement. Negative criticism, on the other hand, is often rooted in negativity or malice. It may be vague, overly harsh, or delivered in a way that is meant to hurt rather than help.

However, even negative criticism can be useful if approached with the right mindset. By filtering out the emotional charge and focusing on any valid points, one can find valuable insights and lessons in even the most challenging feedback. The key is to remain open-minded, objective, and willing to learn from all forms of criticism.

Examples of Transforming Criticism into Success

1. The Beatles: Defying the Odds and Making History

The Beatles, one of the most iconic bands in history, did not achieve their legendary status without facing considerable criticism. Early in their career, when The Beatles auditioned for Decca Records in 1962, the record label famously rejected them, saying, "Guitar groups are on the way out." This harsh criticism could have discouraged them, but instead, it fueled their determination to succeed.

The Beatles did not allow this setback to define them. They continued to practice, refine their sound, and perform relentlessly. Their hard work paid off when they signed with EMI's Parlophone label, and soon, their music took the world by storm. Instead of being deterred by criticism, they used it as motivation to prove their detractors wrong. Their story illustrates that what may initially appear as a failure or rejection can become the impetus for future success when criticism is turned into a driving force for improvement.

2. Rudyard Kipling: From Rejection to Renown

Rudyard Kipling, the acclaimed author of *The Jungle Book*, also faced his share of criticism before achieving success. When Kipling first tried to establish himself as a writer, he received a rejection letter from the San Francisco Examiner that stated, "I'm sorry, Mr. Kipling, but you just don't know how to use the English language."

This criticism was not only harsh but dismissive. However, Kipling did not give up. He continued writing, honing his craft, and eventually became one of the most celebrated authors of his time, winning the Nobel Prize in Literature in 1907. His story exemplifies how one can take even the most negative criticism and use it as a springboard for success. Kipling's perseverance in the face of rejection shows that the strength to accept criticism and continue moving forward can ultimately lead to recognition and appreciation.

3. J.K. Rowling: Turning Rejection into Record-Breaking Success

Few modern authors have faced as much initial rejection as J.K. Rowling, the creator of the *Harry Potter* series. Before her manuscript was accepted, Rowling received numerous rejections from publishers who believed that a story about a young wizard would not appeal to the market. One publisher even advised her to "get a day job," suggesting that she would never make money from writing children's books.

Rather than giving up, Rowling used this criticism as motivation. She continued to revise her manuscript, believing in the value of her story. Finally, Bloomsbury, a small London publisher, decided to take a chance on *Harry Potter and the Philosopher's Stone*. The rest is history—the *Harry Potter* series has sold over 500 million copies worldwide, becoming one of the best-selling book series in history. Her story is a powerful example of how accepting criticism and persisting despite it, can transform the future into a gigantic success.

Her perseverance and belief in her work, even in the face of repeated rejection, led to global success and widespread appreciation.

Turning Criticism into Strength

Criticism, whether constructive or destructive, holds the potential to shape our future for the better if we learn to harness its power. When we learn to accept criticism gracefully, we develop resilience, adaptability, and emotional intelligence. Here are some practical ways to use criticism to build a stronger self:

1. **Listen Without Defensiveness:**

   - When faced with criticism, listen actively and openly. Avoid immediately defending yourself or explaining away your actions. Take a moment to understand the perspective of the person offering the feedback, even if it is uncomfortable.

2. **Seek the Truth in Criticism:**

   - Even in the harshest criticism, there may be elements of truth that can help you grow. Reflect on the feedback and identify any valid points on which you can work. Ask yourself, "Is there any truth in this that I can learn from?"

3. **Respond with Gratitude:**

   - Thank the person offering criticism, especially if it is constructive. Acknowledging feedback shows maturity and a willingness to improve. Gratitude for criticism can disarm critics and open the door for more productive dialogue.

4. **Act and Improve:**

   - Use criticism as a roadmap for growth. Set specific goals for improvement based on the feedbacks you receive.

o   Whether it is refining a skill, changing a habit, or altering a perspective, taking action is key to converting criticism into future appreciation.

5. **Filter Out Negativity:**

   a. If criticism is delivered harshly or with negative intent, focus on the content rather than the delivery. Separate the emotional charge from the message and consider whether there is anything valuable to be gained. Reject personal attacks but embrace constructive points.

6. **Reflect and Reframe:**

   a. Reframe criticism as an opportunity for self-improvement rather than a personal attack. Remind yourself that criticism is not a reflection of your worth but an opportunity to become a better version of yourself.

The Pitfalls of Solely Seeking Appreciation

While appreciation is pleasant and boosts confidence, relying solely on it for validation can be detrimental. When we only accept appreciation, we may fall into the trap of arrogance, believing that we are infallible or beyond reproach. This mindset can create a barrier to growth, as it discourages self-reflection and improvement. It can lead to complacency, where we become content with where we are, rather than striving to reach our full potential.

Appreciation is essential, but without the balance of constructive criticism, it can create a false sense of security. The most effective path to personal and professional growth involves a balance between accepting appreciation with humility and embracing criticism with grace. This balance is important to have in life as it provides the right direction and stability.

The Power of Resilience: Learning from the Greats

The stories of The Beatles, Rudyard Kipling, and J.K. Rowling remind us that criticism is often the first step on the path to greatness. These individuals did not allow rejection or criticism to deter them. Instead, they used it as fuel for their journey, proving that true strength comes from the ability to turn setbacks into steppingstones.

Each story exemplifies a crucial lesson: that criticism can be converted into appreciation with the right mindset and perseverance. The Beatles did not give up when told "guitar bands are on the way out." Kipling did not stop writing because someone thought he didn't know how to use English. Rowling did not abandon her manuscript despite countless rejections. They accepted the criticism, learned from it, and continued moving forward with determination.

Practical Applications and Reflection

Here are some practical steps to help transform criticism into a tool for personal growth:

1. **Invite Feedback:** Actively seek feedback from trusted sources who have your best interests at heart. Encourage them to provide both positive and constructive criticism.

2. **Create a Criticism Journal:** Keep a journal where you record feedback you receive, along with your reflections on it. Note what you can learn from each piece of criticism and what steps you can take to improve.

3. **Practice Self-Compassion:** Understand that everyone makes mistakes and faces criticism. Treat yourself with kindness and patience as you learn and grow from your experiences.

4. **Build a Support Network:** Surround yourself with people who provide honest and constructive feedback. Seek mentors, colleagues and friends who help you see your blind

spots and encourage you to improve.

6. **Celebrate Small Wins:** Recognize and celebrate your progress, even if it is incremental. Every step taken in response to criticism is a step toward growth and future success.

Reflection Questions:

1. Think of a time when you received criticism. How did you react, and what did you learn from it?

2. Are there areas in your life where you tend to avoid or reject criticism? Why, and how can you change your approach?

3. How can you actively seek out constructive criticism to aid your personal and professional growth?

Conclusion: The Journey from Criticism to Appreciation

Accepting criticism and converting it into future appreciation is an art that requires humility, resilience, and a willingness to grow. Criticism is not something to be feared or avoided; it is an opportunity to strengthen our character and enhance our capabilities. The stories of The Beatles, Rudyard Kipling, and J.K. Rowling show us that even the harshest criticism to the level of outright rejection can be a catalyst for remarkable success if we embrace it with the right attitude.

By learning to accept criticism positively, we build a stronger self, capable of turning today's challenges into tomorrow's triumphs. We become more adaptable, resilient, and open to growth. We learn that while appreciation is rewarding, it is the lessons learned from criticism that truly shape us into the best versions of ourselves.

Quote 4

"Use your privileges for making a positive change in other's lives. Abusing them just because you can, and you will only end up harming."

Chapter 4

The Nature of Privilege: Power with Responsibility

Privilege can be defined as a special right, advantage, or immunity granted or available to a particular person or group. It is an unseen benefit that offers opportunities or advantages that others might not have. Yet, privilege itself is neutral—it is how one chooses to wield it that determines its impact. When used wisely, privilege becomes a powerful tool for positive change; when abused, it can cause harm, division, and suffering.

The essence of this chapter is understanding that privilege is a form of power, and like any power, it comes with great responsibility. The challenge is not merely in possessing privilege but in choosing to use it consciously, with empathy and integrity, to uplift others.

Privilege as a Force for Good or Harm

Throughout history, privilege has been both a source of incredible progress and profound harm. When individuals and institutions have used their privileges to uplift, empower, and create positive change, they have left lasting legacies. Conversely, when privileges have been abused for selfish gain, they have led to inequality, suffering, and a breakdown of trust.

Historical Examples of Privilege Used for Positive Change:

1. **Mahatma Gandhi: Privilege for Social Justice**

   o Mahatma Gandhi was born into a relatively privileged family in India. He had the benefit of education, financial stability, and social standing. Gandhi could have lived a comfortable life, but instead, he chose to use his privilege to fight for justice and equality.

- o   After experiencing racial discrimination in South Africa, Gandhi returned to India and leveraged his social standing and education to lead the fight against British colonial rule. He used his privilege to amplify the voices of the oppressed and mobilize millions in a nonviolent struggle for independence. By doing so, Gandhi turned his personal advantages into a powerful force for national freedom and social justice, creating a lasting impact on the world.

2. **Eleanor Roosevelt: Privilege for Human Rights**

- o   Eleanor Roosevelt, the wife of U.S. President Franklin D. Roosevelt, was born into a wealthy and influential American family. Her privilege gave her access to resources, networks, and platforms that were unavailable to most people of her time. Instead of remaining in the background or using her position solely for personal gain, she became a leading advocate for human rights, social justice, and gender equality.

- o   As First Lady, she traveled extensively, meeting with people from all social classes to understand their struggles. She used her platform to speak out against injustice, promote civil rights, and champion the cause of the poor and marginalized. Later, as the chairperson of the United Nations Human Rights Commission, she played a key role in drafting the Universal Declaration of Human Rights, using her influence to promote global standards for human dignity and freedom.

A Personal Example: The Privilege to Heal or Harm

As a surgeon, I am granted a unique and profound privilege—the ability to "violate the integrity of the human body" to repair what is broken. This privilege is both a great responsibility and a delicate balance. In my hands lies the power to make decisions that will impact someone's life in a way few other professions can. I have the authority to make incisions, alter anatomy, and reconstruct what has been damaged—all in the name of healing.

However, this privilege is not without its potential for abuse. The trust patients place in me is immense. They come to me in their most vulnerable states, allowing me to do what would otherwise be unthinkable - cutting into their bodies, exposing their innermost parts, and manipulating their very structure. This trust is sacred, and it is my duty to honor it.

But it is easy to see how this privilege could be abused. There are moments in my career when the temptation to use this power carelessly or selfishly could arise. When faced with pressure from external forces—whether financial, social, or institutional—the line between ethical practice and exploitation can blur. The ability to decide on a surgery or treatment plan could be influenced by motives other than the patient's best interest. This is where the true test of character lies.

The Potential for Abuse: A Cautionary Reflection

I am reminded of a colleague, a talented surgeon who began his career with great promise. He was brilliant, skilled, and ambitious. He knew the intricacies of the human body and could perform procedures that left others in awe. But over time, the pressures of success and the allure of recognition led him to stray from the ethical path.

He started to perform surgeries that were not entirely necessary, convincing himself and his patients that they were. He rationalized his actions by believing he was providing a service, but deep down, he knew that the motivation was driven by financial gain and personal acclaim.

What began as a small compromise, eventually spiraled into a very damaging situation. Patients trusted him implicitly, not knowing that their trust was being manipulated. Eventually, his actions caught up with him. A series of investigations revealed the unnecessary procedures, the inflated costs, and the breach of trust. His reputation was destroyed, and more importantly, many patients suffered unnecessary harm.

This example serves as a powerful reminder of how easily privilege can be abused when self-interest supersedes the duty to care for others. The consequences of abusing such privileges are not just professional but deeply personal—they tarnish the integrity of the individual and harm those who placed their trust in them.

Historical Example of Privilege Abused: The Fall of Enron

The story of Enron, once one of the largest companies in the United States, is a classic example of how the abuse of privilege can lead to widespread harm. Enron's executives were in a position of great privilege, with access to immense financial resources, insider knowledge, and the trust of their employees and investors. However, instead of using this privilege to build a sustainable business, they chose to engage in unethical practices for personal gain.

Through accounting fraud, manipulation of financial statements, and insider trading, Enron's leadership misused their privileges, creating an illusion of profitability while driving the company into bankruptcy. The fallout from Enron's collapse was devastating. Thousands of employees lost their jobs and pensions, investors lost billions, and public trust in corporate governance was severely damaged. This case highlights the destructive consequences of abusing privilege, not just for individuals, but for entire communities and economies.

Using Privilege to Serve: A Commitment to Ethical Practice

My experience as a surgeon has taught me that the privilege to heal must always be balanced with the responsibility to serve with integrity. Every decision I make in the operating room is guided by the principle that I am here to heal, not to harm. I must always ask myself, "Am I doing this for the benefit of the patient, or is there another motive at play?"

When I see a patient on the operating table, I remind myself that this privilege is not mine to wield lightly. I remember the countless hours of training, the sleepless nights, and the moments of doubt that have led me to this point. But more importantly, I think of the trust that my patients place in me, trusting me with their bodies, their futures, and, in many cases, their lives. This trust is a gift—a privilege—that I must honor by upholding the highest standards of care.

Privileges in Everyday Life: Beyond the Operating Room

While the example of a surgeon may seem unique, the concept of privilege applies to all of us in several ways. We each possess privileges, whether they come from our education, our economic status, our social connections, or our positions of influence. The challenge lies in recognizing these privileges and using them for good.

1. **Education and Knowledge:** Having access to education is a privilege. It enables us to learn, grow, and expand our understanding of the world. When used wisely, this privilege can help educate others, create opportunities, and empower those who may not have the same access to knowledge. However, if used solely for personal gain, it can lead to elitism and inequality.

2. **Wealth and Resources:** Financial privilege provides access to resources, security, and opportunities. It can be a powerful tool for philanthropy, community development, and social change. Yet, when wealth is hoarded or used selfishly, it can contribute to social divisions and perpetuate poverty.

3. **Social Influence and Connections:** Being in a position of influence—whether in politics, business, or social circles – comes with a privilege to shape opinions and drive change.

When used for advocacy, justice, and inclusion, this privilege can transform societies. However, when it is used to manipulate, exclude, or exploit, it leads to systemic harm and injustice.

Balancing Privilege with Responsibility

To use privilege wisely, we must constantly balance our power with responsibility. We must ask ourselves tough questions about our motives, our actions, and their impact on others. We must be vigilant against the temptation to use our privileges for personal gain at the expense of others.

One way to achieve this balance is through self-awareness—understanding our own privileges and the contexts in which they operate. Self-awareness helps us recognize when we are operating from a place of privilege and enables us to make conscious choices about how to use that power ethically.

Another way is through empathy and compassion—putting ourselves in the shoes of those who may not have the same privileges. Empathy helps us understand the experiences of others and drives us to use our advantages to uplift, rather than to harm.

The Consequences of Abusing Privilege

History is replete with examples of individuals and institutions that abused their privileges and ultimately faced dire consequences. From corrupt leaders who misused their power for personal gain to companies that exploited their customers and employees, the abuse of privilege often leads to a loss of trust, credibility, and social capital. Abusing privilege can have far-reaching effects, not just on the individual or institution but also on society as a whole. It erodes trust, creates inequality, and perpetuates cycles of injustice and harm. When privileges are abused, they create a ripple effect that affects everyone.

A Call to Use Privilege for Good

Ultimately, the choice is ours. Privileges are not entitlements; they are responsibilities. They are tools that can either build bridges or erect walls. As a surgeon, I have learned that the privilege to heal must always be balanced with the duty to do no harm. The same applies to all of us, regardless of our privileges.

We have the power to make a positive change in the lives of others, to use our privileges to create opportunities, to extend kindness, and to build a more just and compassionate world. But we must also recognize the potential for harm when privileges are misused and commit to using them responsibly.

Practical Steps for Using Privilege Wisely

1. **Recognize Your Privileges:** Reflect on the privileges you possess in your own life. Consider how they have shaped your opportunities and experiences.

2. **Use Privilege to Serve:** Find ways to use your privileges to benefit others. Volunteer, mentor, donate, advocate—there are countless ways to be effective.

3. **Stay Humble:** Remember that privilege is not a sign of superiority; it is a tool that can be taken away or lost. Stay humble and grounded in how you use it.

4. **Challenge Injustice:** Use your privilege to speak out against inequality and injustice. Stand up for those who may not have the same voice or platform.

5. **Commit to Ethical Practice:** Whether in your personal life, your career, or your community, commit to using your privileges ethically and with integrity.

Reflection Questions:

1. What privileges do you have in your life, and how have they shaped your opportunities and experiences?

2. How can you use your privileges to make a positive impact on the lives of others in your community or profession?

3. Are there areas where you might be unconsciously abusing your privileges? How can you change your approach to ensure you are using them ethically?
4. What steps can you take to become more aware of your privileges and their effects on others?

Conclusion: The Responsibility of Privilege

Privilege, whether it is the ability to heal as a surgeon, access to education, wealth, or social influence, is a powerful tool that comes with a great deal of responsibility. It can be used to uplift, heal, and promote justice—or it can be abused, leading to harm, division, and a loss of trust. The choice of how to use privilege rests with each of us, and that choice defines our character and the impact we have on the world.

As we go through life, it is crucial to remember that our privileges are not simply our own to enjoy or exploit; they are opportunities to serve others and contribute to a greater good. Whether on the operating table or in everyday interactions, we must wield our privileges with care, empathy, and integrity.

By consciously choosing to use our privileges for positive change, we create a legacy of compassion, respect, and justice. We become part of the solution rather than the problem, helping to build a world where privileges are not just benefits but responsibilities that everyone takes seriously.

Final Thoughts: Transforming Privilege into Purpose

Imagine a world where everyone used their privileges for good. A world where those with wealth used it to eradicate poverty, where those with influence advocated for the voiceless, where those with knowledge educated the uninformed, and where those with power empowered the powerless. This is the world we can create when we understand the true purpose of privilege—not as something to be hoarded or abused but as a gift to be shared, a tool to be used wisely, and a responsibility to be embraced.

Let us, therefore, commit to using our privileges with humility, empathy, and a clear conscience, always remembering that they are not ours to keep but ours to give. In doing so, we honor the trust placed in us, uphold our integrity, and make a meaningful difference in the lives of others.

Quote 5

"Earn for your work, don't just work to earn."

Chapter 5

The Essence of Rightful Remuneration: Beyond Just Earning

Earning is a fundamental part of human life—it is necessary for survival, comfort, and progress. However, the way we earn, how we achieve our goals, is equally, if not more, important than the earnings themselves. Rightful remuneration, or earning fairly and ethically, is essential to maintaining integrity, building trust, and creating a healthy work environment. When we focus solely on earning money without considering the ethics behind our actions, we risk creating a workplace filled with negative behaviors such as jealousy, one-upmanship, and manipulation.

The Negative Effects of Working Just to Earn

When the sole focus of work is financial gain, several harmful dynamics can emerge within the workplace:

1. **Jealousy and Toxic Competition:**

   o A workplace driven solely by earnings often fosters jealousy among colleagues. When employees are motivated purely by money, they may begin to see each other as competitors rather than collaborators, leading to unhealthy competition and resentment.

2. **Undermining and One-Upmanship:**

   o In environments where financial gain is the primary goal, individuals may engage in unethical behaviors, such as undermining colleagues or manipulating situations to their advantage. This behavior erodes trust, damages relationships, and creates a hostile work environment.

3. **Erosion of Work Culture:**

- A culture centered around earning at any cost often lacks respect, empathy, and collaboration. When individuals are only working to earn, the focus shifts away from the quality of the work, creativity, and shared goals, leading to a breakdown in morale and productivity.

4. **Lack of Respect Among Co-Workers:**

    a. Respect is a foundational element of any healthy workplace. When the focus is solely on earning, respect among co-workers can diminish. This lack of respect can manifest in poor communication, conflict, and a general decline in the quality of work and job satisfaction.

Rightful Earning: The Importance of Ethical Practices

Rightful earning is about ensuring that our work is aligned with ethical principles, fairness, and integrity. It involves recognizing the value of the work we do and ensuring that we are compensated appropriately, while also respecting the value of others' contributions. This mindset fosters a positive work environment, where trust, respect, and collaboration thrive.

Henry Ford - Fair Wages for Fair Work

Henry Ford, the founder of Ford Motor Company, revolutionized not just the automobile industry but also the way businesses viewed employee compensation. In 1914, Ford introduced the "$5-a-day wage," which was more than double the average pay of workers at the time. This decision was groundbreaking and sparked widespread debate across the business world.

Ford believed that his workers should earn enough to afford the products they made. By offering fair wages, he ensured that his employees were motivated, satisfied, and loyal. This decision had several profound effects:

1. **Increased Productivity and Reduced Turnover:**

   o By paying his workers fairly, Ford significantly reduced employee turnover, which was a major problem at the time. Workers were more inclined to stay with the company, reducing the costs and disruptions associated with hiring and training new employees.

   o Higher wages also led to increased productivity. Workers felt valued and were motivated to contribute their best efforts, knowing that their hard work was recognized and rewarded.

2. **Creating a Positive Work Culture:**

   o Ford's decision to pay fair wages fostered a positive work culture where employees felt respected and valued. This culture led to increased job satisfaction, a sense of loyalty, and a collaborative spirit among the workforces.

   o Ford's approach also discouraged jealousy and competition, as employees were motivated by fair compensation and a shared sense of purpose, rather than by trying to outdo one another for personal gain.

3. **Building a Sustainable Business:**

   o Ford's fair wage policy was not just about altruism; it was a strategic business decision. By ensuring that his workers could afford the products they made, Ford expanded his customer base and ensured the long-term success of his company.

   o His approach demonstrated that ethical earnings and fair compensation could lead to sustainable business growth and success. Ford understood that whenever employees are treated fairly & paid rightfully, it goes on to create a virtuous cycle of productivity, innovation, and profitability.

Milton Hershey - Earning Through Quality and Fairness

Milton Hershey, the founder of the Hershey Chocolate Company, built his business on the principles of quality, fairness, and ethical practices. Hershey's story is a compelling example of how a commitment to rightful earning can create a lasting legacy.

1. **Investing in Employees and the Community:**

   o Hershey believed that his employees were his most valuable asset, and he was committed to treating them with fairness and respect. He built the town of Hershey, Pennsylvania, with amenities such as schools, parks, housing, and recreational facilities for his workers and their families.

   o By investing in his employees and the community, Hershey created a loyal workforce that was motivated to contribute to the company's success. His approach demonstrated that fair treatment and ethical earning practices could foster loyalty, increase productivity, and build a strong brand.

2. **Focusing on Quality and Fairness:**

   o Hershey's business model was based on producing high-quality chocolate products at affordable prices. He believed that earning should come from providing real value to customers, not from exploiting them. His commitment to quality and fairness earned him a reputation for integrity and built customer trust.

   o Hershey's success was not just a result of financial acumen; it was driven by his commitment to ethical practices, fairness and respect for his employees and customers. His example illustrates that rightful earning involves a balance between profitability and ethical responsibility.

3. **Creating a Positive Work Environment:**

   o Hershey's approach created a positive work environment where employees felt valued and respected. This environment fostered collaboration, creativity, and innovation. Employees were not just working for a paycheck; they were motivated by a shared sense of purpose and pride in their work.

   o The Hershey Chocolate Company thrived because it was built on principles of fairness, respect, and ethical practices. Hershey's legacy demonstrates that when businesses prioritize rightful earning, they create a culture of trust, respect, and long-term success.

The Value of Ethical Earning: Lessons from Ford and Hershey

The examples of Henry Ford and Milton Hershey provide valuable lessons on the importance of ethical earning and the positive impact it can have on a business and its workforce:

1. **Fair Compensation Builds Loyalty and Productivity:**

   o When employees are compensated fairly for their work, they feel valued and respected. This sense of value fosters loyalty, reduces turnover, and increases productivity. Employees who believe they are earning rightfully are more motivated to contribute their best efforts to the organization's success.

2. **Ethical Practices Foster a Positive Work Culture:**

   o A focus on ethical earning and fairness helps to create a great & positive work culture where respect, collaboration, and integrity are the norms. This culture discourages negative behaviors such as jealousy, one-upmanship, and manipulation, and promotes a sense of shared purpose and community.

3. **Sustainable Success Comes from Rightful Earning:**

   o Businesses that prioritize rightful earning—compensating employees fairly, respecting their contributions, and operating with integrity—are more likely to achieve sustainable success. This approach builds trust with employees, customers, and the community, creating a solid foundation for long-term growth and profitability.

The Importance of Respect Among Co-Workers

Respect among co-workers is a crucial component of rightful earnings. When employees respect one another, they are more likely to collaborate effectively, communicate openly, and support each other's growth. Respect fosters a sense of belonging and unity, which enhances morale and productivity.

1. **Respect Promotes Collaboration:**

   o In a respectful work environment, employees are more willing to share ideas, provide feedback, and work together toward common goals. Collaboration is essential for innovation and problem-solving, and it thrives in an atmosphere of mutual respect.

2. **Respect Reduces Conflict:**

   o A lack of respect often leads to conflicts, misunderstandings, and tension among colleagues. By fostering a culture of respect, organizations can reduce conflicts and create a more harmonious work environment. This undoubtedly goes on to benefit the work place in increasing productivity.

3. **Respect Enhances Job Satisfaction:**

   o Employees who feel respected by their peers and superiors are more likely to be satisfied with their jobs. Job satisfaction leads to higher retention rates, improved performance, and a stronger commitment to the organization.

Practical Steps for Promoting Rightful Earning and Respect

1. **Ensure Fair Compensation:**

   o Organizations should regularly assess their compensation practices to ensure they are fair and competitive. Fair wages are a critical component of rightful earning and help foster a positive work environment.

2. **Promote Ethical Practices:**

   o Encourage transparency, accountability, and ethical behavior at all levels of the organization. Leaders should model ethical behavior and reward employees who demonstrate integrity and fairness.

3. **Foster a Culture of Respect:**

   o Create policies and practices that promote respect among co-workers. Encourage open communication, provide opportunities for team building, and address conflicts promptly and fairly.

4. **Recognize and Value Contributions:**

   o Recognize and reward employees for their contributions, both big and small. Acknowledge the value of each person's work and ensure that everyone feels appreciated and respected.

Reflection Questions:

1. Do you feel fairly compensated for the work you do? How does this affect your motivation and job satisfaction?

2. How can you promote a culture of respect and fairness in your workplace?

3. What steps can you take to ensure that your earning practices are ethical and aligned with your values?

Conclusion: Rightful Earning as a Foundation for Success

"Earning for the work you do" means more than just receiving a paycheck; it means being compensated fairly for one's contributions, working with integrity, and maintaining a focus on ethical practices. When organizations prioritize rightful earning, they build trust, foster respect, and create a culture where employees feel valued and motivated to do their best.

The stories of Henry Ford and Milton Hershey show that businesses built on principles of fairness, respect, and ethical earnings are more likely to achieve sustainable success. By earning rightfully, we not only create a positive impact on our workplaces but also contribute to a more just and equitable society.

Final Thoughts: Earning with Integrity and Purpose

The means of earning matter as much as the earning itself. When we choose to earn rightfully, we build a foundation of trust, respect, and integrity. We create workplaces where people feel valued and motivated to contribute, where collaboration and creativity thrive, and where success is shared by all.

By earning with integrity and purpose, we not only enrich our own lives but also the lives of those around us, creating a ripple effect of positive change that extends far beyond the workplace.

Quote 6

"Buttering your way to the top will inevitably lead to a nasty and slippery fall."

Chapter 6

The Allure of the Easy Path: Buttering and Sycophancy

In the quest for success, some individuals choose a path that seems easier and less challenging: flattery and sycophancy, often referred to as "buttering." This approach involves using excessive praise, insincere compliments, and manipulative behavior to win favor from superiors, rather than relying on hard work, talent, or genuine competence. While such tactics may yield short-term rewards—a promotion, a pay raise, or a coveted position—they rarely, if ever, lead to lasting success. In fact, those who "butter their way up" often find themselves on a slippery slope that leads to a sudden and inevitable fall.

Short-Term Gains, Long-Term Consequences

1. **The Fragile Foundation of Sycophancy:**

   o Success achieved through sycophancy is built on a fragile foundation. It relies on the whims and perceptions of others rather than on one's own capabilities. People who use flattery and manipulation to rise quickly often lack the necessary skills, experience, and resilience to maintain their positions once they reach the top.

   o As an individual advances by ingratiating themselves rather than through merit, they become more vulnerable to changes in management, organizational priorities, or the discovery of their lack of genuine competence. The very foundation of their success is unstable, and any shift can cause it to collapse.

2. **Erosion of Personal Credibility and Respect:**

   o While buttering up may provide temporary rewards

it ultimately erodes one's credibility and respect in the eyes of colleagues and superiors. People who rely on flattery are often seen as lacking integrity and authenticity. They are perceived as manipulative, self-serving, and untrustworthy which are in fact, true.

- o Over time, this reputation becomes a barrier to genuine professional relationships, growth, and opportunities. True respect and recognition come from demonstrating competence, integrity, and dedication—not from manipulative behavior.

2. **Lack of Skill Development and Growth:**

- o Those who choose the path of sycophancy often miss valuable opportunities for personal and professional growth. Instead of challenging themselves, learning new skills, and expanding their knowledge, they focus on maintaining their position through flattery.

- o As a result, they may find themselves in roles or positions they are not adequately prepared for, lacking the skills and experience needed to excel. Their inability to perform eventually becomes evident, leading to their downfall.

The Importance of Faith in One's Abilities

1. **Believing in Your Competence:**

- o True success is built on the foundation of confidence in one's abilities. When individuals have faith in their skills, knowledge, and experience, they are more likely to take on challenges, seek out opportunities for growth & achieve meaningful accomplishments.

- o Believing in oneself means recognizing one's strengths and weaknesses and being willing to put in the effort required to improve and grow. This mindset fosters resilience, adaptability, and a genuine sense of accomplishment.

2. **Earning Respect and Trust:**

    o Success achieved through hard work, integrity, and competence earns respect and trust from colleagues, superiors, and peers. People are more likely to support and collaborate with individuals who demonstrate authenticity, reliability, and dedication.

    o When success is built on genuine merit, it is more likely to be sustainable and rewarding in the long term. The respect and trust earned through competence become a solid foundation for future growth and opportunities.

The Inevitable Fall: A Cautionary Tale of Buttering Your Way Up

Buttering your way to the top may seem like a shortcut, but it is fraught with risks. As the saying goes, "What goes up must come down," and this is especially true when success is built on manipulation rather than merit.

1. **The Slippery Slope:**

    o The imagery of buttering your way up is apt— imagine climbing a ladder covered in butter. With each step, you are trying to gain a foothold not by strength, skill, or determination, but by slippery tactics. One small misstep, one change in circumstance, or one moment of exposure, and you are bound to come tumbling down.

    o The fall is often swift and harsh because there is no solid ground to stand on. Those people who achieve their positions through flattery find it difficult to maintain their standing when their lack of genuine skill or capability is revealed. They slip back down, with little chance of regaining their previous positions.

2. **Case Study: The Downfall of Leaders Who Relied on Flattery**

- o History is filled with examples of individuals who rose to power through manipulation and flattery, only to fall dramatically when their lack of genuine leadership skills or competence was exposed. One example is the case of Niccolò Machiavelli's "The Prince," which describes court sycophants who gained temporary favor but were swiftly removed when their lack of true merit was revealed.

- o In more recent history, many corporate leaders who relied on flattery and sycophancy to ascend to positions of power have found themselves ousted when their inability to perform became evident. Their superficial success was short-lived, and their reputations were permanently damaged.

Example: Adam Neumann and the Rise and Fall of WeWork

Adam Neumann, co-founder, and former CEO of WeWork, provides a striking example of how relying on flattery, charisma, and grandiose promises can lead to a rapid ascent, but an even faster fall. Neumann's meteoric rise to prominence was fueled by his magnetic personality and a bold vision for WeWork, which he pitched not just as a real estate company, but as a revolutionary movement to transform the way people work. Through his charm and persuasive skills, Neumann managed to attract billions in investment, securing the backing of powerful figures like Masayoshi Son of SoftBank.

Neumann created a culture at WeWork where dissent was not at all entertained and only those who flattered and supported his grand vision thrived. Employees and investors were often swept up in his enthusiasm and the hype he generated, which masked significant financial instability and operational issues within the company. However, when WeWork attempted to go public in 2019, the company's financial weaknesses were exposed, revealing excessive losses, unsustainable business practices, and conflicts of interest.

Once the scrutiny of public markets laid bare the company's flawed foundation, WeWork's valuation plummeted from $47 billion to less than $10 billion almost overnight. The very investors who had once praised Neumann's vision turned against him, and he was forced to step down as CEO. Neumann's reliance on charisma and flattery, rather than sound business strategy and competence, led to a swift and dramatic downfall. The company he built faced massive restructuring, layoffs, and financial losses, while his reputation suffered a severe blow.

Neumann's story is a cautionary tale of how buttering one's way to the top—through charm and superficial tactics—can create an illusion of success, but ultimately leads to a nasty and slippery fall when reality catches up. It underscores the importance of building careers and companies on solid foundations of competence, integrity, and sustainable practices, rather than on manipulation or inflated promises.

For Employers: How to Recognize True Talent and Avoid the Pitfalls of Flattery

As an employer or leader, it is essential to distinguish between those who use manipulation and flattery to advance and those who genuinely contribute to the organization's goals. Here are some practical ways to identify genuine talent:

1. **Evaluate Performance, Not Praise:**

   o Focus on measurable outcomes, results, and competencies rather than on compliments or ingratiation. Always keep an eye on those employees who demonstrate consistent performance, creativity, and problem-solving abilities.

- o Regularly review employees based on objective criteria, such as their contributions to projects, teamwork, leadership, and innovation, rather than their ability to please or flatter superiors.

2. Encourage Open Communication:

- o Create an environment where open, honest communication is valued. Encourage employees to speak up, share their ideas, and provide constructive feedback. This practice helps to create a culture of merit and transparency, reducing the influence of sycophantic behavior.

- o Be aware of those who may be afraid to provide honest feedback due to fear of repercussions. Leaders should foster trust by rewarding honesty and discouraging manipulative behavior.

3. Look for Long-Term Commitment and Integrity:

- o Employees who are genuinely committed to their work and the organization's mission are more likely to have long-term success. Look for individuals who exhibit integrity, dedication, and a passion for their work, rather than those who focus on pleasing their superiors.

- o Reward employees based on their integrity, work ethic, and contributions to the company's long-term goals, not on their ability to butter up the hierarchy.

The Power of Authenticity: Building a Sustainable Career

Choosing to build a career based on one's abilities, skills & genuine contributions leads to sustainable success. Here are some reasons why authenticity matters:

1. **Long-Term Stability and Growth:**

   o Individuals who rely on their skills, knowledge, and experience rather than flattery are more likely to enjoy long-term career stability and growth. Their success is based on solid achievements that can be measured, replicated, and built upon.

   o Authentic professionals are more adaptable to changes in the workplace because they are continuously developing their competencies and learning new skills.

2. **Resilience in the Face of Challenges:**

   o Those who have confidence in their abilities are more resilient when faced with setbacks or challenges. Instead of resorting to flattery or manipulation, they focus on finding solutions, learning from their mistakes, and improving themselves.

   o This resilience makes them more valuable employees and leaders, capable of navigating demanding situations and contributing to the organization's success.

3. **Genuine Respect and Influence:**

   o Authentic individuals earn respect and influence naturally because they are seen as dependable, competent, and trustworthy. Their opinions are valued, and their contributions are recognized by peers and superiors alike.

   o Unlike those who rely on flattery, authentic individuals don't need to manipulate their way to the top; their skills and actions speak for themselves, creating a solid reputation that stands the test of time.

Avoiding the Slippery Path: A Call for Integrity

As we navigate our careers, it is crucial to avoid the temptation of taking shortcuts through flattery and sycophancy. While it may seem like an easy path to success, it is fraught with pitfalls and risks that can lead to a rapid and irreversible fall. Instead, we must have faith in our abilities, work diligently to develop our skills, and seek recognition through genuine contributions.

Employers, too, must be vigilant in identifying true talent and avoiding the pitfalls of rewarding superficial behavior. By fostering a culture that values integrity, hard work, and competence, they can build a more sustainable and productive organization.

Practical Steps to Build Authentic Success:

1. **Focus on Continuous Learning:**

   - Invest in your personal and professional growth by constantly learning and improving your skills. Seek out opportunities to expand your knowledge and expertise and stay current with industry trends and developments.

2. **Seek Feedback and Embrace Constructive Criticism:**

   - Regularly seek feedback from peers, mentors, and superiors to understand areas where you can improve. Be open to constructive criticism and use it as an opportunity for growth and development.

3. **Cultivate a Reputation for Integrity:**

   - Be consistent in your actions and decisions. Demonstrate honesty, transparency, and reliability in all your dealings. A reputation for integrity is a powerful asset that will carry you far in your career.

4. **Build Genuine Relationships:**

   o Focus on building authentic relationships based on mutual respect, trust, and shared values. Avoid using flattery or manipulation to gain favor; instead, show genuine interest in others and support their growth.

5. **Set Clear, Values-Driven Goals:**

   o Define your career goals based on your values, passions, and strengths. Align your actions with these goals, and stay committed to achieving them through hard work, dedication, and ethical behavior.

Reflection Questions:

1. Have you ever found yourself tempted to use flattery or manipulation to achieve success? How did you manage it?

2. What steps can you take to ensure that your career is built on a foundation of authenticity and integrity?

3. How can you encourage a culture of merit, respect, and honesty in your workplace?

Conclusion: Building a Career on Solid Ground

"Buttering your way to the top" may be a quick route to success, but those who rely on such methods will face a steep and irreversible fall. True and lasting success is built on a foundation of competence, integrity, and hard work. It holds good not only for self, but even for the ones you hire. By having faith in our abilities, investing in continuous learning, and building our careers on solid, ethical grounds, we can achieve meaningful and sustainable success. As employers and leaders, we must also recognize and reward genuine talent and discourage manipulative behaviors, creating a work culture where authenticity, merit, and respect are the norms.

Final Thoughts: Success through Merit, Not Manipulation:
Ultimately, the choice is ours. We can choose to build our careers as

well as our lives on a solid foundation of integrity, hard work, and genuine contributions, or we can choose the slippery path of flattery and manipulation. One path leads to lasting success and fulfillment: the other leads to a nasty and inevitable fall.

By committing to authenticity and integrity, we ensure that our achievements are not just temporary, but enduring. And when we reach the top, we can stand confidently, knowing that we got there not by buttering our way up, but by earning our place through merit and hard work.

Quote 7

"Judging upon your own perception of things is tomfoolery."

Chapter 7

The Limitations of Judgment Based on Personal Perception

Judging is an ingrained human habit. From the moment we wake up, we assess, evaluate, and judge the world around us based on our experiences, knowledge, and beliefs. However, even the most experienced and knowledgeable individuals can fall into the trap of making incomplete or biased judgments when they rely solely on their personal perceptions. Judging based only on one's viewpoint or limited experiences is like looking at the world through a narrow window—it restricts what we see and limits our understanding of the broader picture.

The "6 or 9" Scenario: An Illustration of Perspective

Imagine two people standing on opposite sides of a number written on the ground. To one person, it looks like a "6," while to the person standing on the other side, it looks like a "9." Both are convinced they are correct, each passionately arguing their point of view. This scenario is a classic example of how our perceptions can be shaped by our position, perspective, or context.

But what if the person who wrote the number on the ground did not intend for it to be either a 6 or a 9? What if it were merely an incomplete doodle that, when seen horizontally, could represent something entirely different? This example demonstrates how judgments based solely on our own perceptions can be not only limited but also misleading. We often fail to consider that our interpretation may not be the only possible truth or even the intended one.

The Dangers of Judging from a Narrow Perspective

1. **Misunderstanding and Conflict:**

- o When we judge based solely on our perception, we risk misunderstanding the intentions, actions, or behaviors of others. Just like in the "6 or 9" scenario, both individuals may feel they are correct, but their limited perspective prevents them from seeing the entire picture.

- o This kind of judgment often leads to conflict, as each person is unwilling to step back and consider the other's viewpoint. The insistence on one's own correctness can escalate minor disagreements into significant disputes, creating unnecessary friction in relationships.

2. Limited Growth and Learning:

- o Judging from a single perspective prevents us from expanding our understanding and learning from others. It confines us to our own experiences and limits our ability to grow. By assuming that our perception is the only valid one, we close ourselves off to the latest ideas, insights, and possibilities.

- o Embracing multiple perspectives enriches our knowledge, enhances empathy, and fosters creativity. It allows us to see things from different angles, recognize the complexity of situations, and make more informed and balanced decisions.

3. Bias and Prejudice:

- o Judging based on one's own perception can easily lead to bias and prejudice. We may form opinions about people, situations, or ideas without fully understanding them. This type of judgment often reflects our own biases, stereotypes, and preconceived notions, rather than objective reality.

o For example, a manager may judge an employee's performance based on their own narrow definition of success, without considering the employee's unique strengths, challenges, or contributions. Such judgments can be unfair and demotivating, leading to missed opportunities and a lack of inclusivity.

The Importance of Empathy and Open-Mindedness

1. **Seeing Beyond Our Own Views:**

   o To avoid the pitfalls of judgment based solely on personal perception, we must learn to see beyond our own views. This requires empathy—the ability to understand and share the feelings of others. Empathy allows us to put ourselves in another person's shoes and consider their experiences, motivations, and perspectives.

   o When we practice empathy, we become more open-minded and less likely to make snap judgments. We learn to ask questions, listen actively, and consider alternative viewpoints before forming conclusions. This approach fosters understanding, reduces conflict, and creates a more inclusive and respectful environment.

2. **The Value of Diverse Perspectives:**

   o Embracing diverse perspectives is essential for growth and progress. When we actively seek out and consider different viewpoints, we gain a more comprehensive understanding of the world around us. This is particularly important in complex or ambiguous situations where there may be no single "correct" answer.

   o By recognizing that our perception is just one part of

the puzzle, we become humble and more willing to learn from others. We open ourselves up to innovative ideas, challenge our assumptions, and become more adaptable and resilient in the face of change.

The 6 or 9: A Deeper Exploration

Let's return to the example of the "6 or 9." Imagine that both individuals are standing on opposite sides of the number, each arguing passionately that they are correct. To the person who sees a "6," it seems obvious that they are right. To the person who sees a "9," their viewpoint also seems irrefutable.

However, what neither person realizes is that their arguments are fundamentally flawed because they are based solely on their individual perceptions. They are so focused on proving their point that they fail to consider that there might be another interpretation altogether. What if the person who wrote the number intended it to be neither 6 nor 9, but rather an abstract symbol, or a simple doodle with no specific meaning?

This scenario illustrates the limitations of judging based on one's own perception. It shows that what we see is not always the complete truth and that there may be multiple valid interpretations of the same situation. To avoid falling into the trap of narrow judgment, we must be willing to step back, question our assumptions, and consider other possibilities. This classically explains the saying – in an argument, there are always 3 sides, mine, yours and the correct one.

A Tale of Two Approaches: The Pitfalls of Premature Judgment vs. the Power of Open-Mindedness

History provides us with countless examples of the dangers of judging too soon and the power of looking beyond one's own views. Consider the contrasting cases of John F. Kennedy and Marie Curie, two figures who faced critical decisions under vastly different circumstances, yet whose approaches offer timeless lessons.

John F. Kennedy, the young and ambitious U.S. President, faced a crucial decision early in his presidency: whether to approve the Bay of Pigs invasion to overthrow Fidel Castro's regime in Cuba. Relying heavily on the advice of a close-knit group of advisors and his own limited perspective, Kennedy judged the operation to be a swift and certain success. However, this judgment failed to consider the complexities of the Cuban situation, including Castro's fanatical support base and the preparedness of his forces. The invasion turned into a disastrous failure, resulting in a humiliating setback for the U.S. and nearly sparking a larger conflict. Kennedy's premature judgment, based on limited views and narrow advice, serves as a cautionary tale of the perils of relying too heavily on one's immediate perspective without seeking broader input or considering alternative viewpoints.

In stark contrast stands Marie Curie, a pioneering scientist who refused to accept the conventional views of her time. Faced with skepticism and outright discrimination due to her gender, Curie chose to look beyond societal prejudices and embrace a unique perspective—that of relentless curiosity and commitment to scientific discovery. Unlike Kennedy, who based his judgment on a narrow set of assumptions, Curie opened herself to new possibilities and ideas, challenging existing scientific norms. Her willingness to look beyond the biases of her era and pursue her passion for science led to groundbreaking discoveries in radioactivity, earning her two Nobel Prizes in different scientific fields. Curie's story exemplifies the power of broadening one's view, remaining open to latest ideas, and resisting the temptation to judge based solely on existing perceptions or societal limitations.

These contrasting examples illustrate a vital truth: while judging from a narrow perspective can lead to disastrous outcomes, looking beyond one's own views can unlock untold potential and lead to extraordinary achievements.

Acceptance and redemption: Thirteen days

While I mentioned the example of John F. Kennedy and the disastrous failure of the Bay of Pigs Invasion, it is crucial to recognize the valuable lesson he learned from this incident, a lesson that would prove vital not just for him but for the entire world during the Cuban Missile Crisis. Over those tense 13 days, the world stood on the brink of a third world war—a nuclear confrontation that could have meant the end of civilization as we know it.

During this crisis, Kennedy chose to go against his initial judgment of adopting an aggressive stance. Instead, he placed a great emphasis on dialogue and negotiation. Despite intense pressure from many of his closest advisors, who were advocating for an immediate invasion of Cuba to destroy the Russian nuclear missile sites being set up, Kennedy remained cautious. These advisors were confident that a surprise attack would be successful, but Kennedy understood that any incomplete military action could easily escalate into a full-scale nuclear war. This was the height of the Cold War, a period when both the United States and the Soviet Union possessed enough nuclear weapons to destroy the world many times over.

Having learned from the failure at the Bay of Pigs, Kennedy's judgment was more measured this time. He decided to involve the United Nations and apply diplomatic pressure on Soviet Premier Nikita Khrushchev. For 13 agonizing days, the world watched as the two superpowers faced off in a deadly game of brinkmanship. Ultimately, Kennedy's decision to pursue diplomacy over aggression paid off—Khrushchev backed down, and the world was spared from the brink of nuclear destruction.

The Role of Experience and Expertise: A Double-Edged Sword

Experience and expertise can provide valuable insights, but they can also be double-edged swords when it comes to judgment. Experienced individuals may feel confident in their ability to judge situations accurately based on their past knowledge and accomplishments. However, this confidence can sometimes lead to over-reliance on personal perception and a dismissal of other perspectives.

1. **The Danger of Overconfidence:**

   o When individuals believe they have seen it all or know it all, they may become overconfident in their judgments. They may assume that their experience gives them a monopoly on truth and become resistant to alternative viewpoints.

   o This overconfidence can lead to errors in judgment, missed opportunities, and poor decision-making. It can also stifle innovation and creativity, as it discourages diverse perspectives and fresh ideas.

2. **Balancing Experience with Openness:**

   o While experience is valuable, it should be balanced with openness to the latest information and perspectives. A wise individual recognizes that there is always more to learn and that their perception is not the only valid one.

   o True wisdom lies in the ability to combine experience with curiosity, humility, and a willingness to consider other viewpoints. This approach leads to more accurate judgments and better outcomes.

Learning from the "6 or 9" Scenario: Practical Applications

1. **Cultivate Humility and Self-Awareness:**

   o Acknowledge that your perception can be just one of

many. Cultivate humility by recognizing the limits of your knowledge and understanding. Be willing to admit when you do not have all the answers and seek out other perspectives.

2. **Ask Questions Before Judging:**

   o Before forming a judgment, ask questions to gather more information. Consider the context, motivations, and perspectives of others involved in the situation. Avoid jumping to conclusions based on limited data or assumptions.

3. **Encourage Open Dialogue and Discussion:**

   a. Foster an environment where diverse opinions are welcomed and valued. Encourage open dialogue and discussion to gain a fuller understanding of complex issues. This approach helps to prevent narrow judgments and promotes a culture of inclusivity and respect.

4. **Practice Active Listening:**

   a. Listen actively to others' viewpoints without immediately forming a rebuttal or counterargument. Focus on understanding their perspective, asking clarifying questions, and reflecting on what you have heard. Active listening promotes empathy and reduces the likelihood of biased judgment.

5. **Challenge Your Assumptions:**

   o Regularly challenge your own assumptions and beliefs. Consider whether there are alternative explanations or interpretations of the situation. Be open to changing your mind when presented with new evidence or insights.

Reflection Questions:

1. Have you ever made a judgment based solely on your own perception? What was the outcome?

2. How can you cultivate a more open-minded approach to understanding others' perspectives?

3. What steps can you take to ensure that your judgments are fair, balanced, and based on diverse viewpoints?

Conclusion: Judging Beyond Perception

Judging based on personal perception alone is tomfoolery. It limits our understanding, creates unnecessary conflict, and prevents us from seeing the world in all its complexity. By recognizing the limitations of our own views and embracing empathy, open-mindedness, and diverse perspectives, we can form more accurate and fair judgments.

The example of the "6 or 9" reminds us that there are often multiple interpretations of the same situation, and what we perceive may not always be the truth. To judge wisely, we must be willing to look beyond our narrow perspective and consider that what you feel may be entirely wrong. Remember, the world was saved when the narrow perspective was changed to a broader one.

Quote 8

"Knowledge of absence is far better than absence of knowledge."

Chapter 8

The Illusion of 'Ignorance is Bliss'

There is a popular saying that "ignorance is bliss," suggesting that not knowing about certain things can make life easier or less stressful. This notion is comforting in its simplicity—if you don't know, you don't worry. But this idea is not only flawed but potentially harmful. Ignorance may provide a temporary sense of peace, but it does not prepare us for the complexities and challenges that life inevitably presents. By ignoring what we do not know, we leave ourselves vulnerable, dependent, and often, at the mercy of circumstances beyond our control.

The Comfort of Ignorance vs. The Cost of Ignorance

Imagine a person who walks along a path every day but never looks beyond the bend. They are content with the familiar stretch they traverse and never question what lies ahead. One day, the path is blocked by a fallen tree, and they have no idea how to navigate around it or find an alternate route. This is the price of ignorance: when confronted with the unknown, we find ourselves unprepared, disoriented, and often overwhelmed.

Ignorance may feel like bliss when things are going smoothly, but it turns into a significant handicap when unexpected situations arise. In contrast, knowing what we do not know—understanding our limitations—allows us to prepare, adapt, and make informed decisions that can mitigate risks and maximize opportunities.

Half-Baked Knowledge: A Double-Edged Sword

If ignorance is a passive state, then half-baked knowledge is an active danger. Knowing a little but believing it to be sufficient very often, leads to overconfidence, poor judgement and lot of misguided actions. This superficial understanding gives a false sense of security that can have grave consequences. The problem with half-baked knowledge is not just that it is incomplete; it is that it blinds us to its incompleteness.

The Dunning-Kruger Effect: Psychologists David Dunning and Justin Kruger coined the term "Dunning-Kruger Effect," which describes the cognitive bias where people with limited knowledge or competence overestimate their abilities. They think they know more than they do and, as a result, make decisions that they are not qualified to make. This effect is particularly dangerous because it leads to errors that could have been avoided with a deeper understanding or a willingness to admit, "I don't know enough."

Examples of Half-Baked Knowledge: The Keto Diet Fad

A prominent example of half-baked knowledge is the popularity of the Keto diet, a high-fat, low-carbohydrate regimen that has taken the health and fitness world by storm. Many people adopt this diet with a superficial understanding that cutting out carbohydrates will lead to rapid weight loss. While this is partially true—limiting carbs forces the body to burn stored fat for energy—this knowledge is only half the story.

The problem with the Keto diet, like many fad diets, is that it entirely cuts out a primary source of energy for the body: carbohydrates. Carbohydrates are vital for fueling the brain and muscles and supporting overall metabolic function. While the diet may lead to swift weight loss initially, it is not sustainable in the long term. Most people who go on the Keto diet eventually experience intense carb cravings, energy crashes, and nutritional deficiencies. When they inevitably return to their regular eating habits, the weight often bounces back, sometimes even more than before.

This phenomenon occurs because many followers of the diet have a half-baked understanding of how nutrition works. They under-stand that reducing carbs can lead to weight loss, but they do not fully grasp the complexities of human metabolism, the importance of balanced nutrition, or the body's need for sustained energy sources. As a result, they make decisions based on incomplete knowledge, leading to poor health outcomes and a cycle of dieting failures.

The Danger of Half-Baked Knowledge

Half-baked knowledge can lead to overconfidence, misguided advice, and decisions that negatively affect oneself and others. It is a risk not just to the individual but also to everyone who may rely on their supposed expertise. To truly understand something, one must be willing to dive deeper, ask questions, and remain open to the latest information.

Acknowledging What We Don't Know: A Path to True Wisdom

True wisdom does not come from knowing everything but from understanding the limits of one's knowledge and recognizing where there is room to learn. This awareness allows for growth and the pursuit of deeper understanding. Socrates, the ancient Greek philosopher, famously said, "I know that I know nothing." This statement was not an admission of complete ignorance but rather an acknowledgment of the vastness of knowledge yet to be explored. It demonstrated humility and a thirst for learning, both of which are essential qualities for personal and intellectual growth.

Understanding the Limits of Knowledge

Knowing that we don't know everything is liberating. It allows us to ask questions, seek answers, and remain curious. It encourages us to become lifelong learners who are always open to new ideas and perspectives. By understanding our knowledge limits, we avoid the traps of arrogance and complacency and remain open to continuous improvement.

The Path to True Wisdom: Expanding the Journey

To truly embrace the knowledge of absence as a path to wisdom, one must cultivate certain attitudes and practices:

1. **Cultivate Intellectual Humility:**

   o Intellectual humility is the recognition that our knowledge is always partial, limited by our perspectives, experiences, and the current state of the world. Embracing intellectual humility means accepting that there is always more to learn, that we can be wrong, and that others may have valuable insights that we do not possess.

   o When we are humble about our knowledge, we are more open to feedback, willing to engage in meaningful dialogue, and less likely to make decisions based on arrogance or overconfidence.

2. **Embrace Curiosity as a Lifelong Companion:**

   o Curiosity is the fuel for the journey of wisdom. It pushes us to explore new ideas, seek out new experiences, and challenge our existing beliefs. A curious mind is always asking questions, always seeking to understand more deeply.

   o Make a habit of asking "why" and "how" about the world around you. Seek new learning opportunities—read books, take courses, listen to experts, and never stop being curious.

3. **Recognize the Value of Diverse Perspectives:**

   o True wisdom comes from recognizing that different perspectives can provide new insights and solutions. Engage with people who have diverse backgrounds, experiences and viewpoints. Listen actively to what they have to say and consider how their perspectives might challenge or enrich your own understanding.

- o By opening yourself to diverse viewpoints, you not only expand your knowledge but also develop empathy and a more nuanced understanding of the world.

4. **Reflect Regularly on Your Knowledge Gaps:**

- o Regular reflection is essential for recognizing the gaps in your knowledge. Ask yourself: What don't I know? Where are my blind spots? What assumptions am I making that could be challenged?

- o Reflection allows you to identify areas where you need to grow and develop, making your learning journey more focused and effective.

5. **Seek Out Mentors and Guides:**

- o Mentorship is a powerful tool for filling knowledge gaps. Identify people who have expertise in areas you are interested in and learn from them. Mentors can provide guidance, share their experiences, and help you navigate challenges.

- o Don't be afraid to ask questions or seek advice from those more knowledgeable than you. Their insights can be invaluable in your journey toward wisdom.

6. **Commit to Continuous Learning:**

- o Embrace a mindset of lifelong learning. Set aside some time regularly, to read, study and

- o explore new subjects. Challenge yourself to step outside your comfort zone and engage with topics that are unfamiliar or even uncomfortable.

- o Remember that learning is not a destination but a continuous process. Celebrate the journey, not just the outcome.

7. **Apply Knowledge Thoughtfully:**

- o Wisdom is not just about acquiring knowledge; it is about applying it thoughtfully and ethically. Use your knowledge to make informed decisions, solve problems, and contribute positively to your community.

- o Recognize that knowledge without application is like a map without a journey—it has potential, but it remains unrealized until it is used.

Filling the Gaps: The Continuous Journey of Learning

Acknowledging our knowledge gaps is the first step toward filling them. But how do we transform this awareness into action? The answer lies in cultivating a mindset of lifelong learning—a commitment to constantly seeking new knowledge, understanding, and skills.

Strategies for Lifelong Learning:

1. **Curiosity as a Driving Force:**

- o Curiosity is the foundation of all learning. Cultivate a mindset that constantly asks questions: "Why?" "How?" "What if?" Let curiosity drive your quest for knowledge. When you encounter something that you don't fully understand, take time, make an effort to explore it fully.

2. **Setting Clear Learning Goals:**

Identify what you want to learn and why it matters to you. Set specific, measurable goals for acquiring knowledge. Whether you aim to learn a new language, master a new software, or understand a complex scientific concept, clear goals will keep you focused and motivated.

3. **Seek Mentorship and Guidance:**

Don't hesitate to seek out mentors or experts in your field of interest. They can provide valuable insights, share their experiences, and help you navigate your learning journey. Engaging with knowledgeable people is one of the fastest ways to expand your understanding.

4. **Embrace a Growth Mindset:**

A growth mindset is the belief that abilities and intelligence can be developed through dedication and hard work. Approach challenges as opportunities to gain experience, rather than obstacles to success. This mindset encourages resilience and persistence in the face of difficulties.

5. **Apply What You Learn:**

Knowledge becomes valuable when it is applied. Experiment with what you've learned, test theories, and put new skills into practice. Real-world applications reinforce learning and provide feedback for further improvement.

6. **Reflect and Iterate:**

Regular reflection is crucial in the learning process. Take time to think about what you've learned, how it applies to your goals, and what adjustments are needed in your approach. Reflection helps consolidate knowledge and identify areas for further exploration.

The Danger of Ignoring What We Don't Know: The Titanic Example

The Titanic's tragic story is a powerful illustration of the dangers of ignoring what we do not know. Built in the early 20th century, the Titanic was celebrated as an engineering marvel. It was designed to be the largest, most luxurious ship of its time, equipped with the latest technology. Yet, beneath the grandeur and the confidence of its creators lay a series of critical oversights—unknowns that would prove fatal.

The "Unsinkable" Myth: The designers and builders of the Titanic believed their ship to be practically unsinkable. This belief was based on the ship's advanced compartmentalized design, which was thought to prevent water from flooding the entire vessel. Confident in this assessment, the ship set sail with fewer lifeboats than needed to accommodate all passengers—just 20 lifeboats for over 2,200 people. The rationale was simple: they did not believe they would need them.

However, this confidence was misplaced. The ship's builders had failed to account for various unknowns: the vulnerability of the steel used in the ship's hull to ice-cold temperatures, the speed at which they were traveling in iceberg-infested waters, and the limitations of their compartmentalized design when multiple sections were breached.

A Series of Ignored Warnings: The Titanic received several iceberg warnings from other ships in the area on the day of the disaster. These warnings were largely dismissed or not acted upon with the seriousness they warranted. The belief in the ship's invincibility blinded the crew to the very real risks ahead. When the ship struck an iceberg, it became clear that the gaps in their knowledge—and their failure to prepare for the unknown—had fatal consequences. Had the ship's designers and operators, acknowledged what they did not know, they might have prepared a a little differently. They could have stocked more lifeboats, reduced speed in dangerous waters, or taken a more southerly route to avoid icebergs altogether. The refusal to recognize their own knowledge gaps led to overconfidence, a lack of preparedness, and ultimately, disaster.

Turning the Absence of Knowledge into an Advantage

Recognizing what we do not know is not a weakness; it is a strength that offers a significant strategic advantage. It allows us to make more informed decisions, seek out experts or mentors, and build stronger, more collaborative teams. It also fosters a culture of humility, empathy, and continuous improvement.

How to Leverage the Absence of Knowledge:

1. **Identify Blind Spots:** Actively seek out and identify areas where your knowledge is lacking. Acknowledging these blind spots allows you to mitigate risks and make better decisions.

2. **Encourage a Learning Culture:** Promote an environment, whether at work or in personal life, where asking questions, seeking knowledge, and admitting gaps is encouraged and valued.

3. **Collaborate with Others:** Use the knowledge of others to complement your gaps. Teamwork and collaboration can significantly expand the collective knowledge base.

4. **Stay Prepared for the Unexpected:** Recognize that knowledge gaps are inevitable and prepare for unexpected scenarios. This could mean planning for contingencies or simply maintaining an open mind about potential outcomes.

5. **Accept when it's clear:** Acceptance is the final step in pushing forwards what you have learnt. It shows commitment to apply the knowledge and skills.

Reflection Questions:

1. What are some areas in your life or profession where you feel you lack sufficient knowledge? How can you take steps to fill these gaps?

2. Have you ever decided based on half-baked knowledge? What was the outcome, and what did you learn from it?

3. How do you typically respond when you encounter a topic or situation you know little about? Are you open to learning, or do you avoid it?

4. What strategies can you adopt to foster a mindset of continuous learning in your daily life?

5. Think of a situation where recognizing what you didn't know helped you make a better decision. How did this awareness impact your choices?

Conclusion: Beyond Blissful Ignorance

Ignorance is not bliss; it is a barrier to growth, progress, and success. Half-baked knowledge, equally, is fraught with danger, leading to overconfidence and misguided actions. The real path to wisdom and achievement lies in recognizing what we do not know, embracing the continuous journey of learning, and striving for mastery in the areas that matter most.

By turning the absence of knowledge into an opportunity for growth, we position ourselves to make more informed decisions, achieve greater understanding, and navigate life with the clarity and purpose provided by our inner compass.

Quote 9

"No decision is good unless you work towards making it so."

Chapter 9

Introduction: The Neutral Nature of Decisions

A decision is a pivotal moment, a choice that sets us on a particular path. Yet, by itself, a decision is neither good nor bad. It is a neutral starting point—a seed that has the potential to grow into something meaningful or wither away, depending on the actions that follow. Decisions are dynamic; they evolve and gain significance only through the work and effort we put in afterward.

Every decision we make opens a door to a series of events. Sometimes the outcomes are foreseeable, and at other times they are shrouded in uncertainty. It is only over time, through consistent effort and adaptive actions, that we discover whether a decision was good or bad. This chapter explores how our work toward achieving the desired results of our decisions is what ultimately determines their value.

Decisions and Actions: The Interdependent Relationship

When making a decision, we often focus on whether it is the "right" one, but the truth is that no decision is inherently right or wrong. A decision is simply the beginning—a choice that points us in a particular direction. The true test of a decision lies in the actions we take afterward and our dedication to pursuing the desired outcome.

Consider a decision like planting a seed. The act of planting is just the first step; whether that seed grows into a healthy plant depends on how we care for it, nurture it, and respond to its needs. Similarly, a decision requires continuous effort, adaptation, and perseverance to bear fruit.

The Importance of Aligning Actions with Goals

To ensure that a decision leads to a positive outcome, it's crucial to determine that subsequent actions align with the desired goals. This alignment requires clarity of purpose and a strategic plan to achieve the intended results. Many decisions fail not because they were inherently bad but because the actions taken afterward were inconsistent or misaligned with the original objectives.

For instance, a business might decide to expand into a new market, which in itself is neither good nor bad. The outcome of this decision depends on how well the company understands the market, adapts its products to local preferences, and executes its strategy. If the actions are well-aligned with the decision, success is likely. If not, the decision may appear flawed, even if it was initially sound.

Harnessing Fire: A Pivotal Decision in Human Evolution

One of the earliest and most transformative decisions in human history was the choice to harness fire. For early humans, fire was a double-edged sword—a source of immense potential and equally great danger. The decision to embrace fire was not made lightly. It involved recognizing the risks: uncontrolled fire could lead to destruction, injury, or death. Yet, the potential benefits were too significant to ignore.

By deciding to control and use fire, early humans unlocked a tool that would fundamentally change their way of life. Fire allowed them to cook food, which made nutrients more accessible and easier to digest, leading to better health and increased brain development. It provided warmth, enabling humans to survive in colder climates and migrate to new territories. Fire also served as protection against predators, illuminating the night and extending hours for productivity and social interaction.

However, the decision to harness fire was only the beginning. Its true value came from how humans chose to use it: carefully managing its power, learning to control it, and applying it to various aspects of daily life. This process required continuous action with a understanding—transforming fire from a raw force of nature into a powerful tool for survival and growth.

The lesson is clear: decisions, like the choice to harness fire, are not inherently good or bad. Their worth is determined by the actions that follow, the commitment to managing the risks, and the persistence to work towards a beneficial outcome.

Example 1: Steve Jobs and Apple's Transformation

Steve Jobs' return to Apple in 1997 is a classic example of how a decision itself is neither good nor bad until the actions following it shape its outcome. At the time of his return, Apple was struggling, facing imminent bankruptcy, and many saw Jobs' comeback as a risky move. His earlier departure from the company had been fraught with controversy, and there were doubts about whether his return would revive Apple or hasten its demise.

Transforming Apple: Decisions as Starting Points

Jobs made several critical decisions upon his return: he streamlined the product line, cutting down on unnecessary products, and focused Apple's resources on a few key areas where he saw potential. He fostered a culture of innovation, insisting on simplicity and excellence in design. However, these decisions were just the starting points. What followed were actions—deliberate, relentless, and visionary actions that transformed Apple from a struggling company to one of the most valuable brands in the world.

- o Focus on Innovation: Jobs' decision to innovate was not simply a declaration but a continuous effort to push the boundaries of technology and design. He introduced the iMac, a product that broke away from traditional designs and appealed to a new audience. The success of the iMac was followed by the launch of the iPod, iPhone, and iPad, which revolutionized their respective markets. It was not the initial decision to return or focus on innovation that guaranteed this success, but the relentless pursuit of these goals through strategic actions.

- o Creating a Unique Culture: Jobs didn't just make decisions at a strategic level; he also worked tirelessly to cultivate a unique culture within Apple. He emphasized simplicity, creativity, and a commitment to excellence, pushing his team to think differently and challenge the status quo. The actions he took to reinforce this culture—such as handpicking his team, setting exacting standards, and personally overseeing key product developments—ensured that the company's vision was consistently pursued.

Results Over Time: Why Actions Matter More Than Decisions

Jobs' return to Apple could have easily been a failure if not for the continuous effort, adaptability, and focus that followed. His decisions to streamline products, foster innovation, and build a unique company culture were necessary, but not sufficient on their own. What made these decisions ultimately "good" was the sustained work, the strategic pivots, and the relentless drive to achieve the desired results.

In this way, Jobs' example illustrates that no decision is inherently good or bad; it is the actions taken to realize the decision that determine its value. The decision to bring Jobs back was validated by the subsequent achievements—Apple's transformation into a technology leader and its creation of groundbreaking products that reshaped industries.

The Role of Time in Validating Decisions

Time is a critical factor in assessing whether a decision was good or bad. Often, it is not immediately clear whether a choice will lead to success or failure. The passage of time allows the consequences of our actions to unfold, revealing whether the decision was wise.

The Importance of Patience and Persistence

Patience and persistence are crucial in decision-making because time often brings unexpected challenges and opportunities. What might seem like a poor decision at one moment could turn out to be the right one if given enough time and effort. It is essential to remain committed to a decision long enough to allow actions to take effect, while also being ready to adapt, as necessary.

Example 2: Elon Musk's Decision to Invest in Tesla and SpaceX

Elon Musk's decision to invest his entire fortune into Tesla and SpaceX is another powerful example of how decisions themselves are neutral and gain meaning through the actions that follow. At the time, both companies were struggling. Tesla faced production delays, cash flow problems, and skepticism about the viability of electric cars. SpaceX was facing technical failures, funding challenges, and doubts about its ability to compete with established aerospace giants.

The Risk of Failure: Decisions Under Uncertainty

Musk's decision to invest his last remaining funds into Tesla and SpaceX was seen by many as reckless and destined for failure. However, Musk's actions following this decision—his willingness to learn from failures, his ability to pivot strategically, and his relentless focus on innovation—were what ultimately turned these companies into successes.

- o Learning from Failures: SpaceX faced multiple rocket launch failures in its early years. Each failure was a test of Musk's decision to pursue the company's ambitious goals. Instead of giving up, Musk used each failure as a learning opportunity, investing time and resources into understanding what went wrong, improving designs, and refining processes. His decision to continue investing in SpaceX was validated by his actions to learn and to adapt, culminating in the company becoming a leader in commercial space exploration.

- o Adapting to Market Conditions: Tesla, too, faced numerous challenges, from manufacturing setbacks to financial crises. Musk's decision to stay committed to Tesla was constantly tested by these difficulties. However, his actions—securing funding, building new factories, innovating with battery technology, and expanding Tesla's market reach—proved that his decision was not reckless but visionary. Over time, his consistent efforts and adaptability turned Tesla into a leader in electric vehicles, proving that the decision to invest in it was a good one.

Commitment to Vision: The Driver of Success

Musk's success with Tesla and SpaceX was not due to the initial decision itself but rather the unwavering commitment to that decision. He believed in the potential of electric vehicles and space exploration and acted consistently toward these goals, despite facing skepticism, setbacks, and immense financial risk. His dedication to working towards making his decisions successful is what ultimately made them so.

Decisions Require Commitment and Adaptability

Decisions, to be deemed good or bad, require a balance between commitment and adaptability. Commitment ensures that we follow through with our chosen path, while adaptability allows us to adjust our course when necessary. The combination of these two elements often determines whether a decision will lead to success.

Commitment: Staying the Course Despite Challenges

Commitment means sticking to a decision even when the going gets tough. It means believing in the value of your choice and being willing to work tirelessly to achieve the desired outcome. It requires resilience in the face of setbacks and the ability to maintain focus on long-term goals.

Steve Jobs' commitment to innovation at Apple and Elon Musk's commitment to technological advancement at Tesla and SpaceX exemplify how sticking to a vision, despite difficulties, can lead to extraordinary outcomes. Without this commitment, their initial decisions might never have borne fruit.

Adaptability: The Key to Navigating Uncertainty

However, commitment alone is not enough. Adaptability is equally important because the path to success is rarely linear. New information, unexpected challenges, and unforeseen opportunities can all impact the outcome of a decision. The ability to adapt—to change tactics, refine strategies, and pivot when necessary—is crucial to turning a decision into a success.

Both Steve Jobs and Elon Musk demonstrated adaptability in their decision-making processes. Jobs adapted Apple's strategies based on market feedback and emerging technologies, while Musk pivoted SpaceX's approach after each failure and adjusted Tesla's business model to meet changing market demands.

Knowing When to Change Course: The Courage to Correct a Decision

While commitment and persistence are essential elements in realizing the potential of any decision, they should not be mistaken for stubbornness or a refusal to acknowledge when things are going wrong. Working toward making a decision successful does not mean achieving the desired outcome "by hook or crook"—by any means necessary, even if it involves unethical practices, denial of reality, or self-destructive actions. Integrity in decision-making is about more than just persistence; it is about knowing when to hold on and when to let go.

Sometimes, despite our best efforts, a decision begins to show signs of failure. The metrics we set to measure progress may start to decline, feedback may become increasingly negative, or new information may emerge that changes the entire landscape of our choice. In these situations, it is crucial to recognize that changing course can be the wisest action. This ability to reassess and pivot is itself a crucial decision that requires humility, insight, and courage.

- o Recognizing the Need for Change: The first step in changing course is to recognize when a decision is turning out to be a poor one. This requires continuous self-evaluation and an openness to feedback. It means asking tough questions: Is this decision still aligned with my goals? Are the outcomes matching my expectations? Am I compromising my values or well-being to achieve this goal? It is only by being honest with us that we can understand when it is time to change direction.

- o The Courage to Pivot: Changing course, especially after investing considerable time, effort, and resources, can be one of the hardest decisions to make. It requires humility to admit that the first decision was not the best one and the courage to take a new path, often into unknown territory. Yet, this is where true decision-making wisdom lies—in the ability to acknowledge mistakes, learn from them, and make a new choice that better serves the intended purpose.

- o Understanding that a New Decision is Also a Decision: Changing course is not a sign of failure; rather, it is an affirmation of the value of making thoughtful decisions. Deciding to pivot, re-evaluate, or completely shift direction shows a commitment to integrity and a willingness to act in alignment with one's goals and values. It is not an abandonment of a decision but a re-commitment to making decisions that are good, just, and true to oneself.

Example of Elon Musk's Willingness to Pivot:

Even successful leaders like Elon Musk have faced moments where changing course was necessary. For example, early in SpaceX's history, several rocket launches failed, putting the company on the brink of bankruptcy. Musk could have continued with the same approach, stubbornly adhering to initial plans, but instead, he chose to re-evaluate, learn from the failures, and make strategic changes. This pivoting and re-evaluation were crucial in transforming SpaceX into a leader in space exploration.

The Real Decision-Making Skill: Knowing When to Change

Decisions are not static; they are dynamic processes that evolve. Part of working toward making a decision "good" is knowing when to reassess, redirect, and even abandon a path that no longer serves its purpose. The decision to change course is not one of defeat but one of strength, wisdom, and commitment to achieving the best possible outcome.

The Myth of the Perfect Decision

Many people fall into the trap of believing that there is a "perfect" decision that guarantees success. This is a myth. There is no single decision that can assure a positive outcome, as every decision carries risks, uncertainties, and unknown variables. The key is to make a well-considered decision and then take the necessary actions to steer it toward success.

The belief in a perfect decision can lead to decision paralysis, where the fear of making the wrong choice prevents any choice from being made. This is often more detrimental than making a flawed decision and working to improve upon it. The focus should be on taking action and making adjustments along the way rather than waiting for the perfect opportunity or choice.

Reflection Questions: Making Your Own Decisions Better

To better understand the concept that no decision is inherently good or bad until you work towards making it so, consider the following reflection questions:

1. Have you ever made a decision that initially seemed poor but turned out well due to your actions? What steps did you take to make it successful?

2. Think of a decision you regret. Were there actions you could have taken that might have led to a different outcome? What could you have done differently?

3. How do you balance commitment and adaptability in your own decision-making process? Are you more inclined to stick with a plan or pivot when faced with challenges?

4. What actions do you take to validate the decisions you make? How do you ensure you are working consistently toward achieving the desired results?

5. Can you think of a time when a decision you made required patience and persistence to prove its value? How did you stay motivated to see it through?

Conclusion: Decisions as Seeds for Action

In conclusion, decisions are seeds that set a course, but they are not inherently good or bad. It is the actions taken to nurture, adjust, and pursue these decisions that ultimately determine their success or failure. Time, patience, persistence, commitment, and adaptability are the essential ingredients that transform a neutral decision into a fruitful one.

Steve Jobs and Elon Musk both exemplify how decisions, followed by relentless effort and adaptability, can lead to remarkable outcomes. There stories remind us well that real work begins after a decision is made. The journey that follows—the actions we take, the adjustments we make, and the persistence we show—is what truly defines whether a decision is good or bad. So, the next time you face a tough decision, remember it is not the decision itself that matters most, but what you do with it. Once you have made a decision, activate your inner compass to help you guide towards making it successful.

Quote 10

"If you have the power, you have the responsibility, but without integrity, they mean nothing."

Chapter 10

Introduction: The Intersection of Power and Integrity

Power is a potent force that can shape destinies, transform societies, and change the course of history. However, power without integrity is like a ship without a compass—it may possess immense potential but can easily veer into dangerous waters, causing destruction rather than progress. Power, when coupled with a deep sense of responsibility and integrity, can become a tool for positive change. Conversely, power devoid of integrity can lead to unimaginable harm and suffering.

In this chapter, we explore the critical relationship between power and integrity. Through historical and personal examples, we examine how the presence or absence of integrity in those who wield power determines whether their actions contribute to the greater good or lead to disastrous consequences.

The Perils of Power Without Integrity: The Example of Adolf Hitler

Few historical figures exemplify the perils of power without integrity more starkly than Adolf Hitler. Rising to prominence as the leader of the National Socialist German Workers' Party (Nazi Party), Hitler was a charismatic orator and a skilled manipulator. He promised to restore Germany's greatness following the economic devastation of World War I and the Treaty of Versailles. However, beneath his promises of revival lay a core of deceit, intolerance, and unchecked ambition that would lead to one of the darkest chapters in human history.

The Misuse of Power: Hitler's Rise and Fall

Hitler's rise to power was marked by a series of unethical actions, propaganda, manipulation, exploitation of public fears, and a ruthless suppression of dissent. Once in power, he quickly dismantled democratic institutions, silenced opposition, and constructed a totalitarian regime based on his racist ideology. His misuse of power culminated in the horrors of the Holocaust, the invasion of numerous European countries, and the widespread suffering and loss of life during World War II.

- o Betrayal of Public Trust: Hitler's use of propaganda to manipulate public opinion is a classic example of power devoid of integrity. He promised economic recovery, national pride, and unity, but his hidden agenda of racial superiority and territorial expansion betrayed the trust of millions who believed in his rhetoric. This betrayal led to the deaths of millions of Jews, Roma, disabled individuals, political dissidents, and countless others in a genocidal campaign that shocked the world.

- o Catastrophic Consequences: The lack of integrity in Hitler's leadership not only caused immense human suffering but also led to his own downfall. The war he initiated resulted in Germany's defeat, widespread devastation, and the division of the country for decades. Hitler's reign ended in a bunker in Berlin, where he took his own life, leaving behind a legacy of destruction. His story is a stark reminder that power without integrity is ultimately self-destructive and brings ruin to all involved.

The Importance of Integrity in Power: The Example of George Washington

In contrast, George Washington, the first President of the United States, offers a powerful example of how integrity can elevate leadership and create a positive and lasting impact. As a military leader during the American Revolution and later as the country's first president, Washington wielded significant power. However he, unlike Hitler, chose to exercise that power with a profound sense of responsibility, humility, and integrity.

Choosing Integrity Over Personal Gain: Washington's Leadership

Washington had numerous opportunities to seize more power for himself. At the end of the Revolutionary War, some of his contemporaries even suggested he become a king. Instead, Washington chose to retire from the army and return to private life, demonstrating his commitment to the principles of democracy and his refusal to exploit his authority for personal gain.

- o Setting a Precedent for Democratic Governance: When Washington was elected as the first President of the United States, he could have easily used his position to consolidate power indefinitely. However, after serving two terms, he voluntarily stepped down, setting a precedent for the peaceful transfer of power. This decision established an enduring tradition of democratic governance in the United States and showed that true leadership requires knowing when to relinquish power rather than clinging to it.

- o A Legacy of Trust and Respect: Washington's leadership was marked by integrity, fairness, and a genuine commitment to the well-being of his country. He prioritized the long-term interests of the United States over his personal ambitions, and his integrity in wielding power helped establish the credibility and stability of the fledgling nation. Today, Washington is remembered not only as a founding father but also as a leader who demonstrated that power, when exercised with integrity, can create a positive and lasting legacy.

Integrity in Crisis: The True Test of Character

Integrity is most critically evaluated during the time of severe crisis.

When faced with intense pressure, leaders may be tempted to compromise their ethics for the sake of expediency or survival. However, it is precisely in these moments that integrity becomes most crucial. Crises often expose the true nature of leadership—revealing whether a leader's commitment to ethical values is steadfast or easily discarded in favor of short-term gains.

Example: Warren Buffett during the 2008 Financial Crisis:

Warren Buffett, known as the "Oracle of Omaha," displayed remarkable integrity during the 2008 financial crisis. As the markets crashed and panic spread, Buffett remained committed to transparency and ethical business practices. Instead of succumbing to fear or opportunism, he chose to make strategic investments, such as in Goldman Sachs, signaling confidence in the American economy. His actions helped stabilize the market and reinforced trust in his leadership. Buffett's integrity during the crisis not only protected his company, Berkshire Hathaway, but also provided reassurance to investors worldwide. Crises are a litmus test for integrity; those who maintain their ethical standards during tough times earn lasting respect and credibility.

Rahul Dravid – Living and Playing with Integrity

Rahul Dravid, one of the most respected figures in the cricketing world, is known not just for his immense talent and dedication on the field, but also for his unwavering integrity. Throughout his cricket career, Dravid embodied the spirit of sportsmanship, playing with grace, discipline, and honesty. He earned the nickname "The Wall" for his dependable and steady presence on the field, but it is his integrity off the field that continues to inspire people around the world.

One of the most telling examples of Dravid's commitment to integrity came when he was offered an honorary doctorate by a prestigious university in India. While many others would have been gleeful and would have gladly accepted such an honor, Dravid declined. He felt that accepting an honorary doctorate would be disrespectful to those who had worked diligently for years to earn that degree through rigorous academic effort. He believed that since he had not made that effort, it would be unfair for him to receive the same recognition.

In his words, "While I deeply respect the institution, I have not earned it in the traditional academic sense, and it would not be appropriate for me to accept it. Those who work hard, study, and make the necessary efforts to achieve a doctorate truly deserve it."

This decision reflects a core aspect of Dravid's character: a deep respect for hard work, fairness, and the achievements of others. He refused to accept a shortcut to recognition, even when it was freely offered. Instead, he chose to honor the integrity of the degree itself and the countless individuals who have dedicated their lives to achieving it through legitimate means.

Dravid's decision to decline the honorary doctorate is a perfect reflection of how he lived his entire cricketing career—with a sense of fairness, humility, and responsibility. He approached every match with the same commitment to hard work and honesty. He never sought shortcuts, and he never placed personal accolades above the spirit of the game or the values he stood for.

His life is a testament to the idea that true integrity means doing what is right, even when no one is watching, and even when it might come at the cost of losing recognition or reward. For Rahul Dravid, integrity is not just a word; it is a way of life. Whether on the cricket field or in everyday life, he remains a shining example of how true character is revealed not only in moments of great triumph but also in the choices one makes when faced with easy gains.

Rahul Dravid's story teaches that integrity requires humility, respect for other's achievements and a willingness to choose the harder right over the easier wrong. His actions remind us that our true legacy is not built on the accolades we receive but, on the values, we uphold and the integrity with which we live our lives.

Personal Example: Choosing Integrity Over Convenience

While historical examples provide valuable lessons, integrity in wielding power is also evident in everyday life. Consider a situation from my own experience when I faced a decision that assessed my commitment to integrity.

Some years ago, I found myself in a financially challenging situation. Despite my best efforts, I needed financial help to tide me over. I already had troubled my extremely supportive parents enough to the point that it was embarrassing. Banks wouldn't lend me because I didn't have enough collateral. It was then that my co-brother, understanding my predicament, extended a helping hand, offering me a loan without interest. It was a gesture of trust, support, and belief in my ability to overcome my difficulties. He didn't even put a timeline on returning the sum.

The Decision Point: Integrity in Financial Choices

When I eventually regained financial stability, I faced a choice: to indulge in the comforts I had long denied myself or to repay my co-brother's loan as soon as possible. While splurging on myself was tempting after a period of hardship, I recognized that my integrity was at stake. The power of choice lay in my hands, and with it, the responsibility to honor my commitments.

I chose to repay the debt first. This decision was not just about financial prudence; it was about maintaining trust and demonstrating gratitude. By choosing to act with integrity, I not only honored the faith my co-brother had placed in me but also reinforced my commitment to my values. In doing so, I affirmed that power—whether financial, professional, or personal—must always be accompanied by a sense of responsibility and ethical conduct.

Power and Integrity: A Delicate Balance

These examples—Hitler's abuse of power, Washington's principled leadership, and my personal decision to repay a debt—highlight a fundamental truth: power and integrity must go hand in hand. Power without integrity leads to destruction, betrayal, and chaos, while power guided by integrity builds trust, respect, and long-lasting positive impact.

Why Integrity is Essential in Leadership

Integrity is the foundation upon which effective and ethical leadership is built. It is what allows leaders to make complex decisions, maintain trust, and inspire others. Without integrity, power becomes a tool for self-serving agendas, manipulation, and coercion. With integrity, power becomes a force for good, driving progress, justice, and positive change.

The Role of Integrity in Decision-Making: Beyond the Quest for Power

Integrity is not just about how one wields power but also about the decisions one makes in any context. It's about aligning actions with values, even when no one is watching or when there are no immediate rewards. A leader's or individual's integrity is revealed not just in grand gestures but in the small, everyday decisions that accumulate over time.

- Consistency in Integrity: Integrity requires consistency in actions and decisions. It is not about choosing to be ethical in one scenario while compromising in another. True integrity is unwavering; it is the ability to maintain a standard of honesty and fairness across all situations, regardless of external pressures or personal gain.

- Integrity as a Measure of Character: A person or leader's integrity is often measured by their commitment to doing the right thing, even when it is difficult, inconvenient, or unpopular. This commitment builds character and shapes a reputation that can have far-reaching impacts beyond any position of power.

Integrity in Everyday Actions: Building a Culture of Trust

Integrity is not only about grand gestures or critical decisions in leadership; it is also reflected in everyday actions. A culture of trust and integrity is built from small, daily decisions made by everyone—from top executives to entry-level employees. These small moments collectively create an environment where integrity becomes the norm rather than the exception.

Example: Ethical Business Practices at Patagonia and The Body Shop:

Patagonia and The Body Shop are renowned for their commitment to ethical business practices and corporate social responsibility. They have built their brand identities around sustainability, transparency, and fairness. Patagonia, for example, prioritizes environmental responsibility by using recycled materials and donating a portion of profits to environmental causes. The Body Shop has consistently championed fair trade and cruelty-free practices. These companies demonstrate that integrity permeates every level of decision-making, creating a culture of trust among employees, customers, and stakeholders. Integrity is a collective effort; it is embedded in everyday actions that, over time, build a strong, trustworthy culture.

Power Without Integrity: Modern Examples and Lessons

Even in recent history, we see numerous examples of how the absence of integrity in leadership has led to downfalls. Consider corporate scandals like Enron or the downfall of political figures who abused their positions for personal gain. These stories highlight that power, when stripped of integrity, is a house on shaky ground.

- Corporate Downfalls: The Enron scandal of the early 2000s serves as a modern example of power without integrity. Executives manipulated financial statements to present a falsely positive picture of the company's performance, deceiving investors, employees, and the public. The lack of transparency, accountability, and ethical behavior led to Enron's sudden collapse, wiping out thousands of jobs, billions in investments, and forever tarnishing the reputations of those involved.

- Political Misconduct: The Watergate scandal that led to President Richard Nixon's resignation is another stark reminder. Nixon's abuse of power, involving illegal activities and subsequent cover-ups, highlighted how even those at the highest level of government could fail if integrity is compromised. His downfall was a significant lesson in the importance of accountability and transparency in leadership.

The Consequences of Power Without Integrity: Key Takeaways

1. Loss of Trust: When leaders or individuals wield power without integrity, they inevitably lose the trust of those they are meant to serve. Trust, once broken, is challenging to rebuild and can have long-lasting negative consequences.

2. Internal Erosion: Without integrity, organizations, institutions, and movements are susceptible to internal conflicts, power struggles, and a lack of unity. The absence of a moral compass leads to decisions based on expediency rather than principles, causing instability and eventual collapse.

3. Moral and Ethical Accountability: Integrity ensures that leaders and individuals remain accountable for their actions. It provides a framework for ethical decision-making and upholds standards of justice, fairness, and responsibility.

The Cost of Compromising Integrity: Understanding the Long-Term Impacts

While short-term gains might tempt individuals or organizations to compromise their integrity, the long-term impacts—loss of reputation, trust, and opportunities—are often devastating. Compromising integrity can offer immediate benefits, but these are fleeting and can ultimately lead to a collapse that outweighs any short-term success.

Example: Elizabeth Holmes and the Downfall of Theranos:

Elizabeth Holmes, once hailed as a visionary entrepreneur in the healthcare sector, compromised integrity by falsifying test results and misleading investors and patients about the capabilities of her company's blood-testing technology. While Theranos initially attracted massive investments and media attention, the truth eventually emerged, leading to the company's collapse. Holmes faced legal repercussions, and the loss of billions in shareholder value serves as a cautionary tale of how deception and lack of transparency can lead to downfall.

Compromising integrity may offer immediate benefits, but the long-term costs far outweigh any short-term gains. True success is built on a foundation of trust, not deception.

Personal Reflection: Integrity in Small Moments

While examples of historical and contemporary leaders offer valuable lessons, integrity also reveals itself in everyday moments—often when no one is watching. It's in the small, seemingly insignificant decisions that one's true character is revealed. Choosing honesty over convenience, fairness over favoritism, or admitting mistakes instead of hiding them are reflections of our core values.

There was a time when I faced a small, yet telling decision. I found a valuable item that someone had lost, and I could have easily kept it without anyone knowing. However, I chose to return it to its rightful owner, even though it required extra effort on my part. This small act was not about gaining recognition but about staying true to my values of fairness and honesty. It reminded me that integrity is built one small decision at a time and that these choices accumulate to define who we are over time.

Reflection Questions: Understanding Power and Integrity

To reflect on the critical relationship between power and integrity, consider these questions:

1. Have you ever been in a position of power? How did you ensure that your actions were guided by integrity?

2. Think of a time when someone wielded power over you without integrity. How did it affect your perception of them? What were the consequences?

3. What actions can you take to ensure that you exercise power—whether in personal, professional, or community settings—with integrity?

4. How can you hold yourself accountable when you are in a position of authority? Are there systems or practices you can put in place to maintain ethical standards?

Consider a leader you admire for their integrity. What specific actions or decisions exemplify their responsible use of power?

Conclusion: Power, Responsibility, and the Unyielding Role of Integrity

The interplay between power and integrity is crucial in shaping our personal, professional, and social landscapes. As we've seen from the contrasting examples of Adolf Hitler and George Washington, the presence or absence of integrity in those who wield power makes all the difference. Power without integrity is a destructive force; with integrity, it becomes a tool for positive change.

Whether we find ourselves in positions of authority in our careers, communities, or personal lives, we must remember that with power comes the profound responsibility to act with integrity. My personal experience of choosing to repay my co-brother's loan before indulging myself underscores the idea that, regardless of the scale, decisions grounded in integrity build trust, strengthen relationships, and contribute to a legacy of respect.

As we navigate life's challenges and opportunities, let us strive to wield whatever power we have with a sense of responsibility, fairness, and unwavering commitment to doing what is right. For in the end, power without integrity is meaningless, but power guided by integrity has the potential to leave a lasting positive impact on the world.

Quote 11

"There are always two destinations when you travel: one that you've planned, and one that you haven't. Spread love and happiness always as the final destination is the one which you've planned for never."

Chapter 11

Introduction: Life as an Unpredictable Journey

Life, at its core, is a journey filled with countless twists and turns, a series of paths we traverse, often unaware of where they might lead us. While we may have clear plans, goals, and dreams for our lives, we must acknowledge that there are always two destinations on every journey: the one we plan for and the one we never expect. Life is a continuous blend of the known and the unknown, the anticipated and the unforeseen.

Each time we embark on any journey—whether it is a physical travel, a new career, a relationship, or any personal endeavor—there is always an inherent risk. Just as every travel brings the possibility of unforeseen events, every moment in life carries with it the potential for unexpected outcomes. We may face accidents, challenges, or an untimely exit from the planet, but what truly matters is the life we live until those moments. A life well-lived should be meaningful not only for us but also for others. It should be filled with kindness, love, and positivity that can leave a lasting impact, regardless of how long or short the journey may be.

Choosing Love Over Hatred: A Path That Heals

In the face of life's unpredictability, we are always presented with a choice: to love or to hate. Hatred is easy; it is a response driven by fear, anger, or resentment. It consumes us from within, leaving behind bitterness and pain. Love, on the other hand, is a conscious choice—a decision to embrace compassion, understanding, and empathy, even when circumstances make it difficult. Love has the power to heal, to bridge gaps, and to create bonds that outlast the harshest storms.

Choosing love in the face of adversity is not merely an act of courage but a deliberate decision to focus on what matters most. It means recognizing that while life may be unpredictable and filled with unforeseen challenges, the journey becomes far more meaningful when we fill it with kindness, generosity, and a commitment to spread happiness wherever we go.

Example: Sheetal Devi – Spreading Happiness Amidst Adversity

One of the most inspiring examples of choosing love and spreading happiness despite extreme adversity is that of Sheetal Devi. Born with a rare physical condition that left her without arms, Sheetal faced unimaginable challenges from the moment she came into this world. Challenges were not for her alone but even her parents. Facing stigma and ridicule over the condition is quite common in many areas of the world. It was no different for her and her family. However, rather than allowing her circumstances to define her, Sheetal chose to defy all odds and embrace life with an indomitable spirit.

Sheetal turned to sports as a means to overcome her physical limitations. She took up archery, a sport that requires precise control, balance, and strength—skills that are difficult even for normal healthy individuals. Yet, with incredible perseverance, courage, and a cheerful outlook, she learned to shoot using her feet. Her dedication paid off as she began winning national and international competitions, becoming a beacon of hope and inspiration for countless others.

But Sheetal's story is not just about winning medals. It is about how she spreads happiness wherever she goes. Despite her physical challenges, she radiates joy, positivity, and love. She encourages others to look beyond their limitations, to find strength in their struggles, and to focus on what they can achieve rather than what they lack. Sheetal's life is a testament to the power of choosing love and spreading happiness even in the face of such great and debilitating adversity.

Her example illustrates that life's journey is not just about reaching a destination. It is about the impact we have on others along the way. Sheetal Devi could have chosen to be consumed by bitterness or self-pity, but instead, she chose to embrace her journey with love, resilience, and a commitment to making the world a better place for others.

Embracing Life's Unexpected Destinations

Every journey we undertake has an element of uncertainty. We may start with a clear destination in mind, but life has its way of surprising us. Sometimes, the detours and unexpected paths we find ourselves on are the ones that bring the most meaning and fulfillment. These unplanned destinations often challenge us, test our limits, and force us to grow in ways we never imagined.

However, embracing these unexpected destinations requires a mindset shift. It means letting go of the need for complete control and being open to whatever life brings. It means trusting that even if the path is difficult, it can lead to growth, learning, and transformation.

The Choice Between Hatred and Love

Life's unexpected twists and turns often bring moments of conflict, frustration, or pain. It is easy to fall into the trap of hatred, blaming others or ourselves for the circumstances we face. Hatred, however, is like a poison; it corrodes our hearts and minds, leaving us drained and depleted.

Choosing love, on the other hand, is like choosing a healing balm. It softens the edges of pain, fosters forgiveness, and brings peace to our hearts. It allows us to connect with others on a deeper level, to understand their struggles, and to find common ground even in the most challenging situations.

Why Loving Even in Adversity is Essential

When we choose love, we choose healing over hurt. We choose to focus on what unites us rather than what divides us. We choose to build bridges rather than walls. Loving in the face of adversity is not only a path to personal peace; it is also a way to create a more compassionate and inclusive world.

Every person we meet on our journey is fighting their own battles, carrying their own burdens. By choosing to love, we offer them a light that can guide them through their darkest hours. We offer them hope, understanding, and a sense of belonging. This, in turn, enriches our own journey, making it more meaningful and fulfilling.

Reflection on Life's Journey: An Inner Travelogue

Reflecting on life as a journey invites us to consider our own paths and the destinations we find ourselves in. It encourages us to ask deeper questions: Are we traveling with love in our hearts, or are we burdened by hatred and resentment? Are we open to the unexpected paths life may take us on, or are we clinging tightly to our own plans and expectations?

Every journey has its challenges, its moments of doubt and despair. But it is in these very moments that we have the opportunity to choose love over hatred, to spread happiness rather than hurt, and to make every destination—whether planned or unplanned— meaningful.

Choosing to Spread Love: A Life Worth Living

Ultimately, the choice is ours. Life will always be filled with uncertainty, risks, and unforeseen challenges. But we have the power to choose how we respond to them. By choosing to spread love and happiness, even in the face of adversity, we create a life that is not only worth living for ourselves but also enriching for others. As we travel through life, let us remember that every moment is an opportunity to spread kindness, to offer compassion, and to leave a positive impact.

Let us choose love over hatred, healing over hurt, and joy over despair. For in the end, the journey itself is all we have, and the love we give is the true measure of its worth.

Reflection Questions: Deepening Your Understanding of Life's Journey

1. Think of a time when you faced an unexpected event in your life. Did you choose to respond with love or hatred? How did your choice affect the outcome?

2. Reflect on a journey in your life where you ended up at a destination you hadn't planned for. What lessons did you learn from this unplanned path?

3. Have you ever encountered someone who radiated positivity despite their challenges, like Sheetal Devi? What impact did their attitude have on you?

4. How can you cultivate a mindset of openness to life's unexpected destinations? What steps can you take to embrace uncertainty with a cheerful outlook?

5. How do you practice choosing love over hatred in your daily life, especially when faced with adversity?

Conclusion: Life's True Destination is Love and Connection

Life's journey is not about reaching a specific destination; it is about the experiences, the people, and the choices we make along the way. It is about how we navigate the uncertainties, how we embrace the unexpected, and how we choose to respond with love rather than hatred.

Whether we encounter planned destinations or unforeseen ones, the greatest fulfillment comes from spreading happiness, kindness, and love. Sheetal Devi's story reminds us that even when life presents us with greatest challenges, we have the power, the ability to choose our response and to make our journey meaningful by uplifting others.

As we continue on our journey through life, let us be mindful of the destinations we reach, both planned and unplanned. Let us strive to leave each place better than we found it, to touch lives with kindness, and to spread love wherever we go. For in the end, the journey is all that matters, and the love we share along the way is the true destination worth reaching.

Quote 12

"The most certain thing in life is still uncertain. Enjoy life because you never know when the uncertainty will become certain."

Chapter 12

Disclaimer: Differentiating the Themes

In the previous chapter, we explored life as a journey with two destinations—one planned and the other unforeseen. We discussed how embracing unexpected destinations can bring meaning and fulfillment. This chapter delves deeper into the inherent unpredictability of life itself and the profound uncertainty that defines every moment of our existence. Here, we focus not only on accepting life's surprises but on living with the understanding that the only certainty in life is uncertainty. The question is not how long we live, but how fully and meaningfully we live each day, making every moment count.

Introduction: Embracing Life's Fundamental Uncertainty

Life is unpredictable by nature. We plan, we prepare, and we work towards certain goals, but the truth is that none of us knows what tomorrow holds. At any moment, our lives can change completely in ways we could never have imagined. This inherent uncertainty is both a challenge and an opportunity. It is a reminder that we have only one life to live, and we must make the most of every moment.

Rather than fearing the unknown or worrying about what lies ahead, we should focus on living fully in the present. We should ask ourselves not "How long have I lived?" but rather "How have I lived?" It is not the length of our lives that truly matters, but the depth and quality of the experiences we have, the connections we make, and the positive impact we leave behind. Our goal should be to live multiple lives within a single lifespan—to seize every opportunity, embrace every challenge, and make a meaningful difference wherever we go.

Living Beyond the Fear of Uncertainty: Choosing to Live Fully

Many people spend their lives fearing the unknown, dreading unexpected turns, and worrying about what might happen next. This fear can hold us back, preventing us from taking risks, exploring new opportunities, and embracing life's full potential. But what if we shifted our perspective? What if we saw uncertainty not as something to fear but as a gateway to endless possibilities?

The unpredictability of life is what makes it so rich and varied. Every day brings new chances to learn, grow, and create. Instead of allowing fear to dictate our choices, we should focus on living fully pursuing our passions, nurturing our relationships, and making positive contributions to the world. It is not about how long we live, but how well we live, and how much joy, love, and purpose we infuse into every moment.

Example 1: Frida Kahlo – Embracing Life Amidst Pain and Uncertainty

One of the most striking examples of living fully despite life's extreme unpredictability is the story of Frida Kahlo, the Mexican painter known for her powerful self-portraits and her vibrant, surrealist art. Kahlo's life was filled with immense pain and uncertainty, beginning with a debilitating accident at the age of 18 that left her with severe spinal injuries and a lifetime of suffering.

Despite her physical challenges and the unpredictability of her health, Kahlo chose to embrace life to its fullest. She painted from her hospital bed, using her art to express her pain, passion, and resilience. Kahlo's work transcended her suffering, capturing the depth and complexity of human emotions. She lived a life filled with love, creativity, and a fierce spirit, making an indelible mark on the world of art and beyond.

Frida Kahlo's story teaches us that even in the face of life's greatest uncertainties, we have the power to create, to express & to live fully.

She did not let her pain define her; instead, she used it as fuel to live more deeply and meaningfully. Her life reminds us that we should not wait for the perfect moment to live fully because such a moment may never come. Instead, we should embrace every day as an opportunity to live multiple lives in one, to make the most of every experience, and to leave a positive impact on the world.

The Courage to Live Amidst Uncertainty: A Call to Action

Living life to the fullest requires courage. It means stepping outside of our comfort zones, taking risks, and daring to explore new territories. It means accepting that there will always be unknowns, and that certainty is an illusion. The only true certainty in life is that it is unpredictable. Rather than letting this reality paralyze us with fear, we should see it as an invitation to make the most of every moment.

Every day, we have the opportunity to make choices that bring us closer to our true selves and to create a life that is rich in experiences, love, and connection. Instead of asking how long we have left, we should ask how many lives we can live within the span of our days. Can we learn new skills, travel to unfamiliar places, form new relationships, and find new ways to contribute to the world? Can we turn every moment into a meaningful one, no matter how uncertain the future may be?

Example 2: Anthony Bourdain – A Life of Exploration and Connection

Anthony Bourdain, the celebrated chef, author, and television host, is another powerful example of someone who lived life to the fullest despite its uncertainties. Bourdain's life was marked by a constant quest for new experiences, new flavors, and new connections. He traveled to the far corners of the globe, exploring diverse cultures, cuisines, and stories.

What set Bourdain apart was his openness to the unknown. What he did was just embracing uncertainty, seeing it as an opportunity to gain experience, to grow, and to connect with people from all levels of society. He believed in the power of shared experiences over a meal, the value of human stories, and the importance of stepping out of one's comfort zone.

Bourdain's life, though tragically cut short, was filled with multiple "lives." He lived as a chef, a traveler, a writer, and a storyteller. He made a positive impact by bridging cultural divides, promoting empathy, and understanding, and encouraging others to explore the world with an open heart. Bourdain's legacy reminds us that it is not the length of our journey that matters, but the richness of the experiences we gather along the way.

Making Every Moment Count: A Life of Meaningful Impact

When we live with the understanding that life is uncertain, we begin to appreciate the value of each moment. We recognize that every day is a gift, an opportunity to have influence, to spread kindness, to learn, to grow, and to love. This awareness prompts us to live more intentionally, to focus on what truly matters, and to create a legacy that extends beyond our lifetimes.

Living fully means making positive changes in the lives of others, whether through small acts of kindness or significant contributions to our communities. It means being present, engaging deeply with the world around us, and seeking ways to uplift and inspire those we encounter.

Example 3: Malala Yousafzai – Standing Up for What Matters Despite Life's Uncertainties

Malala Yousafzai's story is a profound example of living fully and making a significant impact despite the uncertainty and danger that surrounded her. Shot by the Taliban at the age of fifteen for advocating for girls' education, Malala faced an uncertain future filled with threats to her life. Yet, she chose not to retreat in-to fear or self-preservation. Instead, she continued her advocacy with even greater determination.

Malala's courage to stand up for what she believes in, despite the risks, has inspired millions around the world. She lives each day knowing that life is unpredictable, that safety and certainty are never guaranteed. Yet, she focuses not on the fear of the unknown but on the power of her voice and the change she can bring to the world. Her story illustrates that the value of life lies in its meaning and purpose, not in its predictability or length.

Living a Life of Multiple "Lives"

To truly embrace life's unpredictability, we must aim to live multiple "lives" within the single span we are given. This does not mean having multiple careers or identities but rather experiencing life to its fullest by pursuing diverse passions, forming deep connections, and constantly evolving.

- Pursuing Diverse Passions: Whether it is learning a new skill, exploring a new hobby, or starting a new career, living multiple lives means never settling into complacency. It is about continually expanding our horizons and seeking growth opportunities.

- Forming Deep Connections: Every person we meet adds value to our lives. Building meaningful relationships, being open to new friendships, and learning from different perspectives are all ways to enrich our life journey.

- Constantly Evolving: Life is about change, and the most fulfilling lives are those that embrace change with curiosity and openness. Constantly evolving means being adaptable, staying open to innovative ideas, and allowing ourselves to grow from every experience.

Culmination of Learnings: A Reflective Synthesis

This chapter synthesizes all the key learnings from our journey through this book:

- o **Integrity and Purpose:** As we explored in earlier chapters, integrity is fundamental to a meaningful life. Without it, power and success are hollow. Living with integrity means aligning our actions with our values and principles, no matter the uncertainty we face.

- o **Humility and Growth:** Life's unpredictability teaches us humility. It reminds us that no matter how much we achieve, there is always more to learn and room to grow.

- o **Decision and Action:** Decisions are neutral; their value comes from the actions we take to bring them to life. Every decision we make in our unpredictable journey should be followed by purposeful action.

- o **Resilience and Adaptability:** Embracing uncertainty requires resilience and adaptability. It calls us to be flexible, to recover from setbacks, and to see every challenge as an opportunity for growth.

- o **Love Over Hatred:** Choosing love in the face of adversity is choosing healing over hurt. Life's unpredictability offers countless chances to choose love, spread kindness, and are effective.

Reflection Questions: Embracing Life's Uncertainty

1. How can you live more fully in the present, knowing that life is inherently uncertain? What changes can you make to embrace the unknown?

2. Reflect on a moment when your life took an unexpected turn. How did you respond, and what did you learn from that experience?

3. Consider the question, "How have you lived?" rather than "How long have you lived?" What are the multiple lives you have experienced in your journey so far?

4. Who in your life inspires you to live fully and fearlessly despite uncertainty? What can you learn from their example?

5. How can you contribute positively to others, knowing that life is unpredictable? What legacy would you like to leave behind?

Conclusion: Living Fully Amidst Uncertainty

Life's greatest certainty is its uncertainty. We do not know how long we have, but we know that we have this moment. Let us choose to live it fully, embrace the unknown with courage, and make every day a celebration of life. Let us focus not on the length of our journey but on the depth of our experiences, the impact we make, and the love we share.

As you continue on your journey, may you find joy in every unexpected turn, embrace every challenge as an opportunity for growth, and live every moment with purpose, passion, and love. For in the end, it is not how long we live, but how well we live, that truly matters.

Epilogue

A Journey Shared, A Journey Continued

As we come to the end of this book, I want to express my deepest gratitude to you, the reader, for joining me on this journey. Authoring this book has been a deeply personal experience, a reflection of my own life lessons, thoughts, and values. But it is only through your engagement, your reflections, and your willingness to explore these ideas with me that this journey finds its true meaning.

Throughout these chapters, we have touched upon themes that I hope have resonated with you—integrity, humility, decision-making, embracing uncertainty, and living life fully. The reflection questions at the end of each chapter were designed not just to be read, but to be pondered upon, discussed, and shared. They are meant to encourage you to look inward, to challenge your perspectives, and to inspire meaningful conversations with those around you.

I invite you to connect with me and share your thoughts, your experiences, and your reflections. Whether you agree with the ideas presented in this book, find new perspectives, or feel challenged by some of the concepts, I would love to hear from you. Let us continue this journey together—through discussions, debates, and shared reflections, we can deepen our understanding of ourselves and the world around us.

Feel free to reach out to me through social media, email, or any other platform you prefer. Every story shared, and every insight gained adds value to our collective growth. Your voice matters, and I am eager to hear it.

Thank you for allowing me to be a part of your journey. I hope that the words in these pages have inspired you to live with greater purpose, embrace the unpredictable nature of life, and make positive changes wherever you go. May we all strive to live multiple lives within this one, leaving a trail of love, kindness, and integrity in everything we do.

Here is to be continuing the conversation—because every journey is more meaningful when traveled together.

Warm regards,

Dr. Shirish M. Narsapur

Contact Information

E mail – shirishmn@yahoo.com

Twitter (X) - @shirishmn

Telegram - @shirishmn

Instagram - @shirishmn

To know more about Dr Shirish Narsapur's professional Orthopaedic work visit – www.jointsurgeonindia.com

About the Author

Dr. Shirish M. Narsapur is a practicing orthopedic surgeon with a special focus on sports medicine and joint reconstructions. With nearly 20 years of experience in the orthopaedic surgery field, he has developed a unique perspective on life, shaped by both the precision of science and the complexities of the human spirit. His passion for healing extends beyond the operating room, inspiring him to explore deeper questions of purpose, character, and the pursuit of a meaningful life.

As an active member of *Wealthcon* and *Healthcon*, Dr. Narsapur contributes to promoting holistic well-being for doctors, combining physical, mental, and financial health. He believes in the importance of balance and the integration of professional and personal growth. His dedication to helping others navigate life's challenges is evident not only in his medical practice but also in his commitment to fostering resilience and integrity within the broader community.

In his debut book, *The Inner Compass*, Dr. Narsapur shares his quotes, reflections, and stories, drawing from his own life and experiences in the hope of inspiring the readers and to encourage them to live with purpose, authenticity, and courage. He invites readers to connect, reflect, and grow alongside him, finding their own inner compass amidst life's uncertainties.

When he is not in the operating theater or writing, Dr. Narsapur enjoys engaging in thoughtful discussions, especially quantum physics, space & universe, traveling, and continually seeking ways to be inspired from others and also inspire and uplift those around him.

"उद्धरेदात्मनात्मानं नात्मानमवसादयेत्।
आत्मैव ह्यात्मनो बन्धुरात्मैव रिपुरात्मनः॥"

Bhagavad Gita: Chapter 6, Verse 5

"*One must elevate, not degrade, oneself by one's own mind. The mind is the friend of the conditioned soul, and his enemy as well.*"

Notes

Notes

Notes

Notes

Notes

Notes

Notes

Notes